Mark Yaconelli is the co-founder and director of the Youth Ministry and Spirituality Project housed at San Francisco Theological Seminary. His research and ministry with young people has been ground-breaking in its exploration of spiritual direction, contemplation and ancient spiritual practices as the basis of discipleship with young people. Mark is in demand as a retreat leader and speaker throughout the United States. He is married with three children.

T0334559

For Jill:
your love continues to be my deepest experience
of God's grace

and

For Dad:
your passion for life still burns within me.

CONTEMPLATIVE YOUTH MINISTRY

Practising the presence of Jesus with young people

Mark Yaconelli

First published in Great Britain in 2006

Society for Promoting Christian Knowledge
36 Causton Street
London SW1P 4ST
www.spckpublishing.co.uk

Reprinted once
Reissued 2014

Copyright © Mark Yaconelli 2006

All rights reserved. No part of this book may be reproduced or transmitted in any
form or by any means, electronic or mechanical, including photocopying, recording,
or by any information storage and retrieval system, without permission in writing
from the publisher.

SPCK does not necessarily endorse the individual views contained
in its publications.

Scripture quotations are from the New Revised Standard Version of the Bible,
copyright © 1989 by the Division of Christian Education of the National Council
of the Churches of Christ in the USA. Used by permission. All rights reserved.

British Library Cataloguing-in-Publication Data
A catalogue record for this book is available from the British Library

ISBN 978–0–281–07342–9

Typeset by Kenneth Burnley, Wirral, Cheshire
First printed in Great Britain by Bookmarque Ltd, Croydon CR0 4TD

Produced on paper from sustainable forests

Contents

Foreword		vii
Acknowledgements		x
	Introduction: Practising the presence of Jesus	1
1	Teen angst and adult anxiety	11
2	Life without expectations	26
3	Staying alive	37
4	Becoming a good receiver	43
5	Allowing God to love us	50
6	From prayer to presence	64
7	Being with young people	70
8	Remembering	87
9	Forming the beloved community	100
10	The liturgy for discernment	115
11	Noticing	132
12	Naming	151
13	Nurturing	163
14	Beyond fear	176
	Notes	181
	Appendix 1	183
	Appendix 2	187
	Appendix 3	188
	Appendix 4	193
	References	196

This is the first, wildest and wisest thing I know:
that the soul exists, and that it is built entirely
out of attentiveness.

Mary Oliver

Foreword

Several years ago, the Christian Education team at St Andrew's Sunday school found itself floundering. We had been holding classes for children during the regular worship service for years, and while we all felt called to teach our young ones, it was *hard*. We'd figured out a few basic concepts – i.e. children loved to hear Bible stories, loved to talk about them as the stories related to their own lives, and especially loved the arts and crafts projects that illustrated that day's message. We had marvellous curriculum, and we had stacks and stacks of juice boxes.

But there was something missing.

It was sometimes so hard to keep their precious attention. It was hard to impart our love of God to them while letting them be children – with a great deal more physical energy (and needs) than us and with their own eyes through which they were seeing this increasingly scary world.

We read books and consulted a few experts and talked to the children and grew in Jesus, and still we floundered. Our classes usually felt like us-against-them situations, exactly what you don't want in a church school. But *we* were the big people – we made the rules, led the class in prayer, doled out the snacks, attempted to maintain discipline, and tried as well as we could to share the experience, strength and hope we had found in Christ. And *they* were small and fast and fidgety, frequently annoying and wanted to talk about themselves. They sometimes misbehaved and took each other's food and pushed and shoved and all spoke at once. *Ahhh!*

We tried everything, especially prayer. But on bad days the classes were more like babysitting than Christian ministry. We often felt that while we told the kids the most extraordinary faith stories, we still were losing them. We were often frustrated: at one of our meetings I pitched the idea of teachers taking sabbaticals every year (with me being first in line since I'd been teaching the longest and had come up with the idea). We wanted the children to experience the direct love and acceptance of Jesus. More than anything, we prayed we would offer classes that the children really wanted to attend. And just when we got to the end of our rope, our minister found out about Mark Yaconelli.

There was an article in the paper about Mark's highly successful ministry with children and youth, and his belief that children could be a part of – and, in fact, have – their own contemplative ministries. He was teaching teachers and kids how to develop skills to practise the presence of God. He taught teachers how to be with kids in ways that helped them believe that church was a safe place where they could feel fully alive, fully themselves, engaged, listened to, respected and taught, even as they could impart to the teachers their own wisdom and perspective. He was teaching children and teenagers how to be *present* with each other, and with God, in ordinary times, in the midst of messes, and during big and small triumphs. He was making God real, vital, fun, true.

We arranged for him to sit in at our church school one day, and things have never quite been the same at St Andrew's. He started working with children in our classes and in relaxed yet somehow intensive sessions with the teachers. We were invited to watch Mark work with teenagers, and I can honestly say that watching my son Sam get to know Mark has been an experience I cherish. Like every kid who has met him, Sam flipped for Mark. (In fact, one of their conversations is recounted on page 154.)

He taught us how to listen. He taught us how to make classes something we all genuinely look forward to. He helped us become more confident as teachers and more understanding of the fact that the children and youth were teachers too. He shared his deepest spiritual experiences with us, and received ours, with gentle respect. He taught us how to deepen – and help our children deepen – the direct, life-changing experience of the presence of God. There was, of course, always going to be some sense of us-against-them, but as Mark shared the great teachers and writings and voices of Christianity with us, and with the kids, he made the material feel fresh and new again for the teachers and utterly amazing for our students. Instead of us giving our positions on

God and the Bible and spirituality, Mark showed us how to offer young people a chance for authentic spiritual understanding and growth, a chance for joy and safety.

I am so grateful to him, especially for helping my own son look forward to Sundays.

If you are a church school teacher – or a regular parent interested in teaching your own kids – you will find in these pages a wise and patient teacher with a reverence for God, a deep respect for kids, and a lovely sense of humour. You'll find wonderful, hands-on stories about Mark's work with young people, Christian educational leaders, his father, and his own children. There are fantastic tried-and-true exercises for breaking the ice, focusing, and being playful as a group.

Through it all, you will find Mark Yaconelli – and if you are anything like me, you'll find direction and validation and a lot of truly great suggestions in his words.

Finally, I want to promise you that if we can do it at St Andrew's, you can do it, too; and we are doing it now with a much happier sense of purpose, together, on Sunday mornings.

Anne Lamott

Acknowledgements

Since 1993 I have spent hundreds of hours in small circles of people praying, listening and discerning God's presence within churches and youth ministry programmes. This book is just one attempt to put words on the experience and wisdom tended within these little communities of faith.

My first thanks go to the youth who accompanied me as I sought to discover a new way of approaching youth and ministry. Many of these young people were my first teachers in discovering a new way of being with God and others. I'm especially grateful to the youth of St Andrew's Presbyterian Church in Portland, Oregon; Novato Presbyterian Church in Novato, California; and Sleepy Hollow Presbyterian Church in San Anselmo, California, for their patience and friendship as I came to them again and again saying, 'We're going to try a little experiment . . .'

My heartfelt gratitude to those adults with whom I ministered within each of these congregations. Special thanks to Hal Iverson, Terrie Carpenter, Nancy Wiens, Leona Davidson, and Jeff Fletcher from Sleepy Hollow who taught me about ministering as a spiritual community.

The Program in Christian Spirituality and the Diploma in the Art of Spiritual Direction at San Francisco Theological Seminary transformed the way in which I approach God, myself and others. I'm especially grateful to Sister Elizabeth Liebert who continues to be a great mentor, teacher and friend. Thanks also to the PCS community during my years at SFTS – particularly Sister Mary Rose Bumpus, Rebecca Langer, Ann Pope and Joan Currey. Our weekly meetings of prayer, sharing, discernment and planning were invaluable in modelling a new way of working within a religious institution.

This book and the years of research and experience that it rests upon would not have been possible without the foresight of Chris Coble and the generous support of the Lilly Endowment.

Chris saw the potential of contemplative youth ministry long before I did. The subsequent grants given for the creation and support of the Youth Ministry and Spirituality Project allowed these ideas to come to life within youth rooms, congregations and youth ministry institutions across North America. This book is yet another fruit of that investment.

A soul's gratitude to the spiritual directors, scholars, interns, staff and advisers who served within the Youth Ministry and Spirituality Project. Especially Paul Bock, Nancy Wiens, Daniel Wolpert, Garry Schmidt, Teresa Blythe, Diana Cheifetz, Doreen Kostynuik, Scott Hardin-Nieri, Carol Hovis, Marie Pappas, Stephen Iverson and Kay Collette who were involved in several events and consultations. The wisdom and guidance that these spiritual friends provided within the YMSP have transformed me as well as the participants within the project. Special thanks go to the project '*consigliore*' Frank Rogers, whose friendship and guidance have gently tended the work of the Youth Ministry and Spirituality Project, this book and my life.

I am for ever indebted to the youth directors, pastors, churches, denominational leaders and youth who participated in the Youth Ministry and Spirituality Project (1997–2004). The transformation we experienced together was a sign of the reign of God. Special thanks to Tammy Clark and Jen Butler as well as the church leadership and youth ministry communities at Valparaiso First United Methodist Church in Valparaiso, Indiana, and Westminster Presbyterian Church in Eugene, Oregon, respectively, whose commitment to prayer and youth ministry served as a beacon within the project (you can find interviews, testimonies, practices and reports from the folks who participated in the project at www.ymsp.org).

Thanks to Marge and Doug Frank and their colleagues at the Oregon Extension in Lincoln, Oregon, who granted me and my family a place of rest, retreat and reflection where this book could come to life. Thanks to Kirk Wulf, Deborah Arca Mooney, Cory Maclay, Jen Butler, Frank Rogers and Jay Howver who read and 'contemplatively' critiqued the first version of this manuscript.

I am indebted to Andy Dreitcer for his companionship in co-founding and co-directing the Youth Ministry and Spirituality

Project (1997–2000). Andy's wisdom and mentorship were invaluable in the development of my own understanding of contemplative ministry. I carry deep gratitude for Michael Hryniuk, who served as Co-Director of YMSP from 2001 to 2004. Michael's friendship, prayer life, patience and laughter are woven within my life and work.

Deborah Arca Mooney served as programme manager for the YMSP and has been administrative assistant, spiritual director, youth leader, janitor, secretary, cheerleader, nursemaid, travel agent, proofreader, counsellor, concierge, van driver, ego masseuse and mother superior not only to the participants of the project but most especially to me. I cannot imagine engaging this work over the past eight years without her care and friendship.

I owe a 'life debt' to Morton Kelsey (1917–2001), my friend, teacher and spiritual grandfather. His love and acceptance continue to reveal to me the companionship of Jesus.

In 2003 I suffered the loss of my dad, Michael Yaconelli, who was a great playmate, soul friend and colleague. He has been the inspiration within much of my life and ministry and was a great supporter of my exploration of contemplation and ministry. This book is both a response to and a continuation of his life and work.

My heart's gratitude to my family – the little spiritual community that lives with me, eats with me, carries my burdens, celebrates my breakthroughs, offers me forgiveness and enlarges my soul.

Noah, Joseph and Grace: you are my greatest delight. Thank you for your patience while I typed on the computer.

Jill, my one true love, thank you for carefully reading and editing this book as well as most everything I've written since I was 18 years old. I know it's possible to be lovingly and truthfully present to others because I continue to receive this from you. My heart is yours.

Introduction:
Practising the presence of Jesus

The more we receive in silent prayer, the more we can give in our active life. We need silence to be able to touch souls. The essential thing is not what we say, but what God says to us and through us. All our words will be useless unless they come from within. Words which do not give the Light of Christ increase the darkness.

(Mother Teresa of Calcutta)

Young people can't just have somebody reciting lines or reading a book or teaching. You want someone who's learning, someone who's alive and growing with you. That's how you learn that you're on a spiritual journey with somebody. It doesn't work if that adult is at the end of the journey tugging on a rope trying to get you to come along. A young person needs to know you're right there with them. A young person needs to see that you're vulnerable – that you're struggling too. I have to say I haven't seen a single adult enter our youth ministry and leave the exact same way they entered. Everybody has changed . . . and that's just how it's got to be.

(Nathaniel, age 15, Atlanta, Georgia)

Youth are not blank slates, and Christianity is not words. This may seem obvious until you seek to share the Christian faith with young people. Then you may notice that your first impulses involve words. 'What will I say? What books should I read? What answers will I give? What discussion should I encourage? What blanks within young people need filling?' In sharing the faith with young people, most of us think about the words and the empty spaces. If we go to seminary or step inside a Sunday morning worship service we're immersed in words. A newcomer to these settings might easily assume that Christianity *is* words. It's reading, memorizing, lecturing, preaching and writing. It's books, newsletters, worship bulletins . . . words, words, words.

But the central problem in sharing the Christian faith with young people doesn't concern words; it's deeper than that. The real crisis facing those of us who seek to share faith with youth is this:

> We don't know how to be with our kids.
> We don't know how to be with ourselves.
> We don't how to be with God.

We don't know how to be with our kids. We know how to entertain them, market to them, test them and statistically measure them. But we've forgotten how to *be* with them. As a result, today's youth have become more and more isolated, alienated and left to fend for themselves within the molesting arms of the corporate media culture. This isn't just my opinion – it's the conclusion of every major study on adolescent development for the past 15 years.[1] Just listen to Cara Miller of the Search Institute, possibly the largest researcher of adolescent development and behaviour in North America:

> Study after study in the field of youth development makes it clear that the single most important thing that can make a positive difference in the life of a young person is the presence of a caring adult. In spite of that, research shows that most young people don't have enough caring adults in their lives.[2]

Sadly, our absence from the lives of young people is connected to a deeper problem: *we don't know how to be with ourselves.* Most adults are busy. We have no down-time. We move from activity to activity, with few real relationships and little introspection. We're 'distracted from our distractions by our distractions' to para-phrase T. S. Eliot. The result is that we've become 'dis-spirited'. We live narrow lives. We tend to act as if we're nothing more than our roles and our jobs. We become what Thomas Merton calls 'the false self'. Anthropologist Angeles Arrien relates that in many indigenous cultures, a dis-spirited or dis-connected person is diagnosed by asking four questions:

> Where in your life did you stop singing?
> Where in your life did you stop dancing?
> Where in your life did you stop telling stories?
> Where in your life did you stop listening to silence?

When I look at the world around me, I see very little singing that isn't play-listed, very little dancing that isn't connected to soft drinks, very little story-telling that isn't violent and disjointed, and a complete absence of silence. The sad truth, if we're willing to be honest, is that youth are being raised in a culture of people who no longer live from the centre of their lives. The results are catastrophic for those of us who seek to tend the spiritual lives of teenagers. Anyone who befriends young people knows they're people of spirit – people drawn to song, dance, story and silence. We cannot hope to touch the hearts of young people if we have lost our own spiritual rooting.

In the Christian community there is an even deeper block: *we no longer know how to be with God.* In the church we love to debate God, defend God, protect or promote God. We talk to God, praise God, and even serve God. The one thing for which we have little time or patience is actually spending time with God. If you're a pastor in a church, one sure way to get fired is to set aside ten minutes of silence during a worship service for people to just 'be' with God. Try this a few times and soon the church leadership will be inviting you to just 'be' somewhere else.

Increasingly, it appears as if we in the Church have forgotten how to be in relationships – which is tragic, since our primary calling as Christians is to be people of relationship. Jesus calls us to love God with all of our hearts, minds, strength and spirit, and to love others as we love ourselves (Mark 12.29–31). Most youth ministers are drawn into this work by a deep ache to live as spiritual people and to share the life of Jesus with teenagers. To be a spiritual guide you have to spend time in the Spirit. You have to slow down and live at 'God's speed', you have to be patient, give yourself permission to pray, to listen to people, and to be humble and willing to wait on the Holy Spirit to lead the way. How can we share God if we're too busy to be with God? How can we love kids if we aren't present to them?

In contrast to our lives of spinning isolation is Jesus' life of relationship and presence. It's Jesus' presence, his capacity to love and be with people that's transformative. It's the way he listens, shares food, spends time, weeps, walks, touches, responds and cares for people. Jesus enjoys being with people. He enjoys being with God. His ministry, it seems, doesn't come from a pre-planned formula but instead arises in response to the real situations and relationships he encounters.

If we want our young people to live lives of faith we need to live into the presence of Jesus. If the Christian faith is to offer any light, love or truth to young people, we have to move beyond words. We have to seek to share not only the teachings of Jesus, but more importantly the presence of Jesus.

What does it mean to be present? To be present is to be open and available to others with as much of ourselves as possible, as unguarded as possible. To be present is to seek to be awake to the Mystery of God within each moment. It means to relate to youth the way Jesus related to people – authentic and transparent.

For Christians, being present means practising the presence of Jesus. Jesus is generous, patient, kind, welcoming, courageous, truthful and compassionate. Jesus is available to people. He is attentive to God and to others in the present moment. He receives people. He has patient eyes that see people in their beauty as well as their pain. Jesus trusts people. He trusts our capacities to bear love. He trusts us with the good news. He trusts us with life. He trusts that we know more of God than we realize. He says, 'I no longer call you servants, I call you friends . . .' He doesn't say, 'Let me explain . . .' He says, 'Remember . . .' He says, 'Those with ears to hear . . .' He says, 'A sower went out to sow . . .' He says, 'Listen . . .'

The best way to know the presence of Jesus is to turn to him yourself. Who would we become if we spent time in the presence of Jesus? How would we live if we spent long periods of time with someone who trusts us, enjoys us, listens to and cares for us? Who would our young people be if they were companioned by adults who embodied such love and attention?

Most of us can't answer these questions, because we have rarely experienced such presence in our own lives. If we went through our lives and added up the amount of time spent in the presence of another person who truly listened and cared for us, it might equal less than 30 minutes. Yet Jesus demonstrates that this kind of patient presence is possible – and then goes on to tell us that we have the capacity to share this kind of presence with others. He calls us to love one another – and for young people today (and really all of us), love means being there.

Unfortunately, for many young people the last place where they find people open and available is within churches. Instead of a listening ear, they find advice. Instead of a witness to their lives, they're offered programmes and activities. And yet we know that the people who have had the greatest impact on our lives, the people who have changed and shaped us, are the people who were present to us – people who received us in the midst of our pain as well as our breakthroughs.

If we want our kids to grow into themselves, to be people who know how to offer God's love, life and creativity to a brutal, hurting and stunted world, then we need to share the presence of Jesus with them. We need to remember how to be in relationship. Like Jesus, we need to stop and allow ourselves to rest in God. Adults need to spend time remembering how to be with young people.

A contemplative approach to youth ministry

In recent years there has been a rediscovery of the significance of presence within the Christian life. Locked away within ancient books, monastic communities and the lives of individual praying Christians is a deep concern for presence – presence to God as well as presence to other people. This yearning to be fully awake and alive, the desire to be attentive to others, the longing to be receptive to God in every moment of our lives, is the heart of the contemplative tradition.

There are many ways to describe what is meant by *contempla-tive*. But in the simplest language, contemplation is 'being' with God within the reality of the present moment. Contemplation is about presence. It's about attentiveness – opening our heart's eye to God, ourselves and others. Contemplation is an attitude of the heart, an all-embracing hospitality to what is. Contemplation is a natural human disposition – it's the way in which we approached the world as children: vulnerable, open and awake to the newness of the present moment. We have all experienced being contem-platively present. Even as our adult minds become distracted and burdened with worry, we still receive times of contemplation, times of simple presence. These are unrehearsed moments when a deep sense of gratitude falls upon us and we find ourselves without need or want, satisfied and reverent at the Mystery of life. It's moments when we feel surprisingly alive to the people and situ-ations before us. Like love, contemplative awareness is not some-thing we achieve; rather it comes as a gift, simply to be received.

Ignatius of Loyola referred to contemplation as 'seeing God in all things'. Brother Lawrence called it 'the pure loving gaze that finds God everywhere'. Jean Pierre de Caussade defined contem-plation as 'the sacrament of the present moment'. Teresa of Avila referred to this experience as 'awareness absorbed and amazed'.

My favourite description is from Walter Burghardt, who said contemplation is 'a long loving look at the real'. In contemplative youth ministry we are seeking to look, long and lovingly, at what is. Contemplative youth ministry is about seeking courageously to behold the reality of our own lives, the reality (whether it be joy or suffering) of the young people we serve, and the reality of God's love beneath it all.

These definitions of contemplation, I believe, are descriptions of how Jesus was present to others. He engaged people with openness and honesty, unafraid to take 'a long loving look at the real' – at the people and situations he encountered.

Contemplative youth ministry is an invitation to slow down and receive the young people in our lives. It's a reminder that what young people need most are people who know how to be present to God and present to others. What would it be like if our ministries were filled with adults who took 'a long loving look at the real'? How would our youth respond if adult Christians engaged youth with patience and transparency? What would it mean for our own lives if we could become people who sought to be present and receptive to what God brings us in life instead of hurriedly striving towards the next task or project?

To be attentive to youth and aware of God in the present moment is always a struggle. We live in a complex age that demands that we multi-task. We grow up trained to attend to many times and places at once. Our own minds and imaginations often drift toward the future or dwell in the past. And yet is there any greater gift we experience in this life than the gift of another person's full attention? Is there anything more loving than to be fully seen and heard by another? Didn't most of us become Christians when we sensed that God was present to us?

Contemplative youth ministry isn't another model competing with other ministry models; it's an opening of the heart, an attentiveness to God, a receptivity to the Holy Spirit, a growing relationship with Jesus and his way of compassion. Contemplative youth ministry isn't about becoming mystics or turning kids into cloistered monks and nuns; it's about helping kids become alive in Christ. It isn't about candles and labyrinths, it's about youth and adults becoming present and available to God's love.

Contemplative youth ministry is an attempt to honour the desire to listen as well as teach within our interactions with kids. It's an effort to ground our ministries in prayer as well as evangelism; in silence as well as in acts of justice. Contemplative youth ministry is about refusing to be so busy that you overlook God within your ministry. It's remembering that Jesus goes before and beside us.

The contemplative tradition of the Christian faith comes to us as a precious gift in an age when no one has time to sit still. It comes as a medicine to a church culture obsessed with trends, efficiency, techniques and bullet-point results. It comes to us just as Jesus came to his disciples in the midst of a busy ministry, asking them to 'come away for a while'. Contemplative youth ministry is about trusting unashamedly that God desires our presence more than our activity. It's about recognizing that, unless we find rest in God, we will continue to live lives that are harried, depleting, and a counter-witness to the life we seek to share among young people.

*　　　　*　　　　*

The ideas and practices presented in this book do not come from detached study; they emanate from my relationships with young people, parents, youth ministers and congregations across North America. For seven years I was given the resources from the Lilly Endowment and San Francisco Theological Seminary to create and co-direct the Youth Ministry and Spirituality Project.

From 1997 to 2000 we gathered a diverse group of churches from across the United States to see what would happen when contemplative prayer and presence was intentionally practised within ministries with youth. These 16 churches and the people who represented them came from 10 denominations encompassing socioeconomic, ethnic, cultural and geographic diversity. They also spanned diverse theological backgrounds – from conservative evangelicals, to Roman Catholics, to liberal Protestants.

Over the first three years of the project we held four, one-week sessions in which we presented to pastors, youth pastors (both paid and volunteer), and at least one other adult from each sponsoring church many of the principles and practices found in this book. In addition to these formation weeks, we also held one-week contemplative formation retreats involving youth from the participating churches.

In 2000–2003, we trained a group of 13 exemplary churches as well as the national youth ministry officers from 10 denominations to become teachers of contemplative youth ministry. These churches and institutions were asked to integrate contemplative youth ministry into their ministries and organizational structures as well as begin to share the insights of contemplative youth ministry within their respective communities.

It has been an enormous privilege to work with so many diverse and gifted congregations. This book is one attempt to pass on some of the insights and transformation that flowed from our efforts to explore a different way of sharing Jesus' message of love with young people. At the beginning of each chapter and within the text I have presented just a small sampling of the stories, testimonies and practices that grew out of the Youth Ministry and Spirituality Project. I urge you to hear these quotes and stories as if you were listening to a dear friend. Notice what words or images stand out to you. See if you can sense the transformation that these parents, youth pastors, church members and pastors have undergone as they have begun to listen more deeply to young people and to the presence of God in their midst. Similarly, I have included many of the exercises and contemplative processes tested within the project. I hope you'll take time to engage the exercises and practices as they are presented in this book – these experiences are critical to understanding its message.

*   *   *

Although I have spent 16 years studying, teaching and practising youth ministry, I must confess that I was never involved in a youth ministry programme when I was an adolescent. The church I attended as a young person was small and rural. It had neither a youth group nor Sunday school classes. What it did have, however, was a time during each worship service in which people were invited to stand and greet one another. This time of greeting was always (and still is) the longest period of the service, as people took the time to hug and converse with every other person in the room. Each Sunday, whether I was sulking in the back row, hiding in the kitchen or immersed in my conversations with friends, people found me, asked how I was, listened to my words and hugged me to their chests. I know I'm a Christian today because those people were present to me during my adolescence. They listened openly to my questions, received me, looked at me with wonder and saw within me a unique revelation of the presence of God.

This book is born of my hope to provide every young person with a handful of adults who incarnate the love, compassion and presence of Jesus in a similar way. I pray that our churches might be filled with adults willing to move beyond words and ministry programmes – adults willing to take the time to seek out the young people in their communities, to sit with them, to listen to them. May every congregation be filled with adults who view the young people in their lives and communities with the eyes of Jesus, beholding in each and every young person a unique revelation of the presence of God.

1

Teen angst and adult anxiety

In our age everything has to be a 'problem'. Ours is a time of anxiety because we have willed it to be so. Our anxiety is not imposed on us by force from outside. We impose it on our world and upon one another from within ourselves.

Sanctity in such an age means, no doubt, travelling from the area of anxiety to the area in which there is no anxiety or perhaps it may mean learning, from God, to be without anxiety in the midst of anxiety.

(Thomas Merton, *Thoughts in Solitude*)

I've really begun to understand what deeply spiritual people teenagers are (silly to have forgotten, when I was one myself). Even the scruffiest middle schooler is on a seriously beautiful, completely unique journey, as we all are, and have been, even when we were little kids. Understanding that has perhaps been the best fruit that contemplative prayer has yielded in my relationship with young people.

(Melissa Range, poet and youth ministry volunteer,
Oakhurst Baptist Church, Decatur, Georgia)

Teenagers make adults anxious. They just do. Spot a group of young people standing on a street corner and most adults get suspicious; pass a group of teens outside their own neighbourhood and they get worried; and if a young person happens to paint their lips black or jump a skateboard off the church steps, adults can get downright fearful. Adult anxiety toward teens is ancient, even biblical. In the only scene we're given from Jesus' adolescence, the young Messiah sneaks away from his family and hides out in Jerusalem. When his mother finally rushes into the temple and discovers her holy middle schooler, she cries frantically, 'Child, why have you treated us like this? Your father and I have been searching for you in great anxiety!' It turns out that that even the teenage Prince of Peace can make adults crazy with worry.

There are many reasons why adults get anxious around teens. Young people are fidgety. They fiddle with things and won't stay still. They exaggerate and mirror adult postures that make grown-ups self-conscious and uncomfortable. They always seem to be looking for something – a friend, an adventure, a ride, food, acceptance, a glimpse of who they're becoming. A young person can look at an adult and voice a question with such open-hearted honesty that you find yourself blushing. Sometimes their neediness or suffering can be obvious in a way that leaves adults feeling helpless or despondent.

Young people are green. They can make adults feel tired, musty and unattractive. Emerging from childhood, teens move toward adulthood with fresh eyes and energy. They see white elephants. They ask the obvious and un-faced questions: 'Why do we have to go to church when Jesus never did?', 'How come you tell me not to drink alcohol when you have a beer every night?', 'Why are these benches called pews?' Just the presence of young people within a community of adults exposes weaknesses, raises doubts and challenges assumed values.

Young people can be disturbingly (or is it refreshingly?) unpredictable; one moment they seem happy to conform to their parents' wishes and adult conventions, the next day it appears they're making it up as they go along, led zig-zag by an internal drummer that even they don't seem to recognize. Young people can express a childlike dependency one moment, then get offended by the lack of independence they're granted the next. Youth are messy. Take the following example.

Three years ago while travelling on a bus full of young people I noticed I was surrounded by five or six teenage girls. At the time, my wife and I were expecting our first daughter and I was eager to learn about relationships between fathers and teenage daughters. I turned to the young girls seated near me and asked if they would be willing to tell me about their relationships with their fathers and to offer any advice they thought helpful. Although these young women were from all over North America and represented diverse ethnic and racial backgrounds, I was surprised at how this particular group spoke in very similar, adoring tones about their dads. Then one 15-year-old said, 'Well, you have to be prepared that there will be times when your daughter might say to you, "I hate you, Daddy!" Then usually by the next day you'll get a hand-made card that says something like, "You're the greatest dad in the world".'

I looked at her bewildered and asked if any of them had enacted this kind of behaviour with their own fathers. Except for one, they all nodded in agreement. I was incredulous. I asked them to tell me what had prompted them to use such extreme language. One girl replied, 'Well, it can be anything really. Like, a couple of months ago I stopped talking to my dad after he wore black socks and sandals to pick me up from school . . . but other times I've said similar things for really no reason at all.' When I asked them why, they just shrugged their shoulders. 'It's just something we do,' one of them offered. Youth make adults anxious.

One thing that becomes increasingly disturbing for grown-ups is a sense that they have little control over young people. This scares adults. Adults want youth to conform to adult standards. They want youth to act responsibly. They want them to sit down and listen. They want youth to hurry up and get their identity fixed and grounded. Adults want youth to have a roadmap for a secure and reasonable future and they get rattled when they notice that most youth aren't carrying one.

Youth make youth directors worry. We don't know what they look at on the Internet, we can't keep up with the electronic gadgets they play with, we've never heard of the bands or celebrities they talk about, we don't know what they do after school, we're unaware of the subject or codes in their e-mail conversations. Over time even the most hip of youth ministers can feel like she doesn't understand young people.

Perhaps one source of adult anxiety is the growing separation between youth and adults. For the past 40 years economic policies, changes in social norms and a relentless marketing strategy to create and sell to a teenage market has combined to create what sociologist Christian Smith calls a 'structural disconnect' between adults and youth.[3] This separation begins long before adolescence. Youth spend most of their childhoods segregated in daycares and schools, afternoons and evenings in front of televisions and computers, weekends hanging out with friends. By early adolescence most young people are attuned to a different reality, a different world than adults.

When youth are segregated from adults they begin to appear more and more mysterious. Adults can fall into projection, speculation, worry and fearful imaginings. Congregations and church leaders find themselves relying on the media to learn about kids. Adults absorb stories about teenage gangs and violence. They watch videos and movies that portray young people as hormone-driven and sex-crazed. They hear news stories and government reports that talk alarmingly about 'at-risk' kids. All of this becomes a filter for how young people are perceived. Adults see teenagers in baggy jeans and oversized jackets and fear they're hiding drugs or weapons. They see a group of young women in short halter tops and lipstick and worry about their sexual activity.

Sadly, most adults are unable to see the real truth – that drug use and sexual promiscuity have continually *decreased* over the past 20 years among young people. So much so that Bill Strauss, co-author with Neil Howe of *Millennials Rising: The Next Great Generation*, claims, 'Never before has there been a generation that is less violent, less vulgar, less sexually charged than the culture being offered them.' We fail to recognize that it's the adult culture that is far more 'at risk' than young people. We are unable to perceive this truth. As Strauss claims, 'We need a youth committee on adult drug abuse, not the other way around.' Instead, we believe the story the media and culture tell us about youth. We don't take the time to get to know our youth as they are in reality. Through the media lens youth are no longer our children, they are no longer people; instead they are a dangerous tribe, a marauding cluster of 'at-risk' statistics evoking fear and apprehension.

Sometimes adult fears about young people arise out of what they *do* know. Adults get scared when young people reflect behaviours and attitudes that they recognize. Adolescent desires for pleasure, material goods, entertainment gadgets, constant activity, sex and even mood-altering substances all mirror the behaviour of the adult culture – and it scares adults. There is much adults don't like about themselves. There are mistakes parents have made and want their kids to avoid. Adults get frightened when young people begin to reflect the ambiguous values and conduct of the adult culture.

I remember a mother of a teenager in my church youth group who was terrified that her daughter was going to start smoking. She brought her daughter to the church in hopes that she would get involved with 'good' kids and healthy activities. She obsessively questioned me after every retreat and camp event to see if her daughter had been smoking. The reason she was scared was that she began smoking in high school and even as an adult was unable to stop the habit. Often the things we as adults fear most in our young people are the issues we haven't resolved in ourselves. As Thomas Hines, author of *The Rise and Fall of the American Teenager* writes, we fear youth because 'we want them to grow into healthier, wealthier and wiser versions of ourselves'. When they don't appear to be on that path, adults get scared.

Maybe what's most unsettling about young people is the way in which they remind grown-ups of their own adolescent heart. Youth can stir up forgotten dreams and evoke unmet longings within adults. Youth can unearth the contradictions between the hopeful vision of our younger selves and the mediocre and muddled reality of our adult lives. Whatever the particular cause, the truth is that when adults relate to teenagers out of anxiety, they miss seeing them, they miss hearing them and they lose their sense of compassion.

Anxiety is the inability to be present. It's a state of agitation in which we lose our larger capacity to empathize, to love, to respond to the needs of others; when we're anxious we become squirrel-like, nervous and wary, teeth chattering, eyes scanning for danger, muscles spring-loaded, waiting to scamper up the nearest tree at every sound. Anxiety comes from words that denote 'to choke'. When we're anxious we can't breathe. We feel life closing in, leaving fewer and fewer choices. We find ourselves unable to discern real fears from reactive worry. We lose patience, we're unable to trust. We get suspicious, distancing ourselves from others, ourselves and even God. We become lost in our heads, caught up in fearful thoughts and calculations. Our minds oscillate between the future and the past – we worry about what should have happened or fear what might take place. In anxiety we lose touch with what's driving us. Our actions become self-protective, reactive and compulsive.

It would be an overstatement to say that anxiety is the only adult response to young people. There are many instances when a young person's presence can be an unexpected grace lifting a grown-up's spirit like a sudden gift of flowers. Youth can be unabashedly friendly and welcoming in a way that wipes away the cloud of mistrust or dourness that many adults live behind. Young people are often playful, drawing energy and new life to the surface of adult lives and communities. Young people can be passionate about God and ultimate meaning in a way that elevates or even carries the faith of those around them. They can authentically embody a heartfelt compassion for suffering and marginalized people that can be revelatory to adults. They can ask the hard question that helps adult communities to see hidden problems or possibilities.

And there are many more positive as well as just plain ordinary human ways in which adults respond and relate to young people. And yet, the primary reaction to teens within Christian communities and the culture at large seems to be anxiety.

The result is that most ministries with youth in the West are ministries of anxiety. In fact, most Christian communities don't even consider the spiritual needs of young people until there's a critical mass of anxious adults. Look behind most youth ministry programmes and you'll find pastors and church boards nervous about declining memberships, parents afraid their kids lack morals, congregations worried that the Christian faith has become irrelevant to younger generations, and the persistent frustration among adults that something ('anything!') needs to be done with 'those kids'! To be unaware of adult anxiety toward youth is often to misperceive what drives most youth ministries.

Teen angst

Of course, adults aren't the only ones with anxieties. Maybe the second most common reason why youth ministries exist is that in equal proportion to adult anxieties about youth is teenage anxiety about adults. Adults make teenagers anxious. They just do.

Once, while facilitating a rite of passage for a group of graduating high school students, I asked the young people to give me their impressions of adulthood. For the next hour kids told stories concerning their observations and experiences with parents, teachers and various adults in the community. As the discussion began to wind down I handed out paper and pencils and asked the youth to craft a one-sentence definition of adulthood based on our sharing. There was silence for a minute or two as the young people began to write and reflect on what they had heard. I then asked the young people to share what they had written. The first young man to respond said, 'Well, as I heard our conversation and thought about my own experiences of adults I wrote this definition: "Adults have no friends, adults have no passions and adults are stressed out."'

Adults have no friends, adults have no passions, and adults are stressed out. After 14 years in youth ministry this young person was able to articulate the fear that I felt among most young people. More and more it appears to me that this is the nightmare of adulthood that most young people are trying to escape. Is it any wonder that there are 30-year-olds living in their parents' house still trying to make it in a rock band? Maybe they're trying to hang on to their friends? Maybe they're trying to keep their passions alive? Maybe they see the grey-suited adults working in cubicles, burdened with responsibility, and they get frightened?

Young people are about energy; they have bodies that want to move, they have emotions they want to express, and they have developing relationships that are incredibly interesting and important to them. Adults – especially in a faith community – want young people to listen, to behave, to be still, to stop talking, to soothe adult fears, to fulfil mission statements and support programmes. This makes young people wary and anxious.

I was once interviewed for a youth ministry position at a

church. Part of the interview was done by a group of young
people who, when I asked them what kind of youth ministry they
envisioned, said things like, 'Something that's not boring', 'Lots of
trips and retreats', 'We want to be able to hang out with friends',
'Lessons about real stuff that we care about – not just what adults
care about.' As they continued to talk, I sensed that behind their
comments were fears, many of them not unfounded, which if
listed would look like this:

- Fear the church wants youth to be passive.
- Fear youth programmes will be about meeting the needs of the adults.
- Fear the real purpose of youth ministry is to make youth 'nice'.
- Fear the youth ministry will be a form of babysitting.
- Fear there will only be talking and no action.
- Fear the ministry will be another activity in which youth have no voice.
- Fear the ministry will have nothing to do with real life.
- Fear young people will have to hide their real thoughts, fears, desires and experiences.
- Fear youth will become as muted, controlled and stressed as the adults in the congregation.
- Fear there is something in Christianity that really matters and yet will remain hidden.

The anxieties and fears that young people hold in regard to
adults and churches are real. Yet ministries that respond only to
teenage anxiety will mimic the media's frenetic activity that seeks
only to keep the attention of young people, without any concern
for the growing hunger of the adolescent soul.

God makes us anxious

There is an even deeper adult anxiety than the ones I've mentioned that impacts our ministries with youth. It's the real and
natural fear that the Christian faith is really about risk, about
breaking free, about becoming vulnerable to the suffering in the
world, about living as an open-hearted person.

A few years ago I was invited to a session meeting for a local Presbyterian church to talk about youth ministry. Instead of my normal presentation I asked the adults to tell me why they started coming to church. Surprisingly I found that almost all of them began attending church once they had children. They began attending church because they thought it would be good for their kids. They wanted the church to help their kids learn the values and morals of the Christian faith. As we talked further we realized that all of them were repeating the same practices as their families of origin. All of the session members had come from families that began attending church when they were children, and then left the church once they had reached late adolescence. I asked them how this had affected their own lives. There was silence. Then one adult said, 'Well, it didn't have much of an effect . . . except once I became a parent I thought I should probably start taking my kids to church.'

I went on to explain that simply taking their kids to church or youth group would probably garner the same results. I explained that the purpose of youth ministry isn't just to help young people learn morality, as important as that is; it's to help them enter into the alternative way of life that Jesus offers. It's to help young people unmask the principalities and powers that seek to bind us, to help them live into freedom. It's to help youth learn the practices, understandings and disposition that will keep them close to the Source of life revealed in Jesus Christ.

'Well, that's all well and good,' offered one parent, 'but I think that's more than we're after.' Heads nodded around the room. 'I think we just want our kids to . . . you know, learn the Ten Commandments, and be kind to others . . . the kind of values Jesus was promoting.' 'Yes,' chimed another session member, 'we don't need our kids to be Jesus, we just want them to participate in the church.' I paused, and then told them that if they wanted their kids to learn morals they would have taken them to a scouting programme. I asked them if maybe there wasn't a deeper desire within their decision to bring their kids to church. I tried to explain that the purpose of the church was to help people live the Christian faith and the Christian faith wasn't focused on morality. The Christian faith is about following Jesus, it's about falling in love with God. It's about seeking to become so transparent to the Spirit of God that you were no longer sure which actions were your own and which ones were God's. I tried to explain that youth ministry wasn't really about church memberships – it was about helping kids live into the freedom and compassion of Jesus. Morality was simply a by-product of loving God and bringing this love out into the world!

I sensed that the adults were curious but didn't know how to respond. People looked down in embarrassment. I became embarrassed. The pastor cleared his throat and in a voice that hinted, 'OK, we've had enough out of you!', he said, 'Yes, terrific! Thanks so much for your words of encouragement. I think we're done here and need to move on to the next item on the agenda.' He then stood and escorted me to the door.

It's so difficult for those of us in the Church to admit that Jesus came to offer us another way of life – a way of life that's more than being a good citizen, more than obeying the law, recycling your garbage and attending church on Sunday. Although we try to ignore Jesus' life of passionate freedom and relationship, the witness of Jesus is not overlooked by the young.

Years ago I was singing to my sons, Noah age four and Joseph age two, as I tucked them in bed. This was a song I had learned as a boy and contained the word 'Christian'. My son Noah, listening to me sing, suddenly asked, 'Dad, what's a Christian?' A panic quickly came over me. This was an important opportunity to share my faith! I needed to proceed carefully. I reviewed all the strategies in which I'd been trained: Testimony? No, too long and I'd risk putting him to sleep. Exegesis on Philippians 2? Might be too heady and I'd have to go into a historical–critical description of Pauline theology, not to mention the concept of kenosis and atonement theologies. Maybe a brief historical sketch of the Council of Nicaea, culminating with a pictographic version of the Nicene Creed? Could be complicated.

My son interrupted, 'Well Dad, what does it mean?'

Before I could gather my thoughts I found myself blurting, 'Well, Noah, it means "little Christ". People who are trying to live like Jesus call themselves Christians.'

Noah paused, pondered this definition and then said, 'Are you a Christian?'

'Yes, I am,' I replied.

Noah stood still, thought for a moment and then said, 'How do you become a Christian?'

I explained that you simply say to God with all your heart, 'I want to join Jesus in loving you and loving others'; and then you try and live your life like Jesus.

Noah thought this over and then said, 'OK, let's do it.'

We sat together on his bed and prayed a simple prayer while two-year-old Joseph jumped and tumbled behind us.

We brushed teeth, read a bedtime story and lay down for sleep. The boys soon became quiet and began to drift into slumber. Then, just as I went to get up Noah said to me, 'Dad, I don't think I want to be a Christian.'

I paused, surprised he was still awake. 'Why is that, Noah?' I whispered.

'Well, Jesus gets killed by the soldiers, doesn't he?'

'Yes . . . he does,' I said hesitantly. Then with calm assurance offered, 'But God raises him and his Spirit is still with us today.'

'I know that, Dad . . . but I don't want to get killed.'

Silence.

'Don't worry,' I said, rubbing his back, 'you're not going to get killed. That happened a long time ago.'

He yawned and with eyes closed said, 'Yes. But if Jesus is still with us today it can happen again.' Pause. Yawn. 'I don't think I want to be a Christian, Dad.'

'OK, Noah,' I said, brushing his hair. 'OK.'

Noah realized that being a Christian has consequences. That living a life of love often results in suffering. That being like Jesus doesn't mean simply being nice and having good morals – it often means facing the pain and evil in the world. And I realized that night why many people resist the real purpose of youth ministries. That night I wasn't sure if I wanted my kids to be Christians to 'pick up their cross and follow Jesus'. The truth is that many parents and adults don't want their young people to 'be like Jesus'. I understood that night why many adults and youth simply want youth ministries that provide morals and safe social activities, without all the weird stuff about growing into the image of Christ. It's difficult to trust our children to God. Look what happened to Jesus! Look what happened to the disciples! Look what happens to his friends, those we point to as saints! Parents, church members and youth might want Christian values and assurances, but don't want the life of Jesus.

Jesus makes us uncomfortable, causes us to question our daily practices. Jesus' life reminds us of the realities of life, the reality of suffering, the hostility, hatred and resistance that often accompany any attempts at living in truth and love. To invite our kids to live into the Spirit of Jesus means they may no longer fit in. It means they may choose to become outcasts. It means they might begin to have compassion for others. They might become vulnerable to the pain and loneliness of the world. It means they could be drawn to live life on the margins. It's not safe to be a Christian: you can lose your life, it can make you an outcast, and it can break a parent's heart.

And yet, as I reflected on my interaction with Noah, I realized that there is a worse fate than facing the suffering and violence of this world. I realized that more than keeping Noah safe from harm, I want Noah and all my children to live. I want them to become fully alive. I want them to know Jesus so that they will know how to keep their hearts soft. I want them to know God so that they'll be intimately connected to the Source of life. I want them to be Christians so that they'll know how to give and receive love; so that they'll avoid the burned-out life of materialism that can deaden their spirit and kill their creativity. And yet, I have to admit, all of this scares me at some level.

A friend of mine who is a youth minister and a committed Christian called me one evening after receiving a phone call from her college-age son. She sounded distressed as she told me that her son had decided to leave his studies in order to join a group of Americans who were going to Iraq to be with Iraqi civilians during the American bombing and occupation. The hope was that by being a visible presence as American citizens they might be able to protect the lives of civilians as well as increase awareness about the suffering of Iraqis back in the US. My friend was upset and told her son that he had made a commitment to college and that this was no time to engage in radical politics. I asked her how her son responded. She sighed; there was quiet over the phone line for a moment. Then she said with tears in her voice, 'He said, "But Mom, this isn't politics. This is about following Jesus. We're going as a Christian group. Didn't you and the church teach me that Jesus was always befriending people who were weak and suffering?"' I waited in silence. I could hear her crying. Then finally she said, 'He's right you know, Mark. I know he's right. But if I knew he was going to do something like this I would have taken him out of the church and raised him to be a Chippendale dancer.'

Rooted and grounded in anxiety

In response to the anxiety of adults (they're the ones with the power after all) most congregations create youth ministries that are about control and conformity. When we're anxious we want control, we want answers, we want concrete and measurable results, we want ducks in a row. In youth ministry this means that most adults want programmes and professionals. Church leaders want experts and predictable systems that will remove the doubt and ambiguity that surround most interactions with young people. Congregations want discipleship formulas that will guarantee that their kids will become moral and faith-filled believers.

When youth ministry responds to the anxiety of adults it becomes restrictive and deadening. God's freeing presence and the at-risk life of Jesus are downplayed in order to conform kids to the tradition, practices and doctrines of the congregation. Soon the youth ministry loses its ability to discover something new, to question and embrace the pain and suffering of life. Ministry with youth becomes safe, revolving around answers and false assurances. The youth are quarantined. They're placed at the margin – incubated in basements or gathered off-hours when the congregation won't be disturbed. The ministry becomes more and more unreal, causing those young people who won't conform to either become disruptive or stuff their real questions and struggles.

Some youth ministries are created in response to *adolescent* anxieties. Noticing young people's discomfort with adult forms of faith and desperately seeking to keep youth engaged, some churches develop ministries of distraction. Inspired by para-church youth ministries from the 1950s like Youth for Christ and Young Life, whose founder Jim Rayburn once wrote a book entitled *It's a Sin to Bore a Kid*, ministries of distraction keep young people moving from one activity to the next: rafting trips, pizza parties, game nights, ski retreats, beach fests, music festivals, amusement parks, taco-feeds, scavenger hunts, crowd-breakers, raves, skits and whatever other activities attract kids. This is the Nickelodeon approach to youth ministry, appealing to kids' propensity for fun and recreation. This is how churches respond to young people who cry, 'Church is boring!' It's the ministry of excitement; discipleship through fun, culture-friendly, 'Christian-light' events. Like parents of a toddler who pop in a video when relatives arrive, the idea is to keep the young people from running out, keep them in the general vicinity of the church, keep them happy until they're mature enough to join the conversation.

Ministries that simply respond to adolescent anxieties often become ministries of diversion, providing virtual environments with virtual relationships that keep youth distracted from the deeper rhythms and practices of the Christian faith. Programmes and activities are chosen based on the level of excitement that's generated. No one wants to act like an adult for fear of scaring the kids. Leaders become hesitant to engage youth in any activity that is in contrast to the consumer culture. Prayer, spiritual exercises, theological conversation and spiritual disciplines that challenge the *status quo* are dumped, fearing youth may cry: 'This is like school!' or 'You're just like our parents!', or worse: 'This is boring.' And so the ministry never addresses the deeper needs of the youth, never challenges young people to explore the alternative way of Jesus. Like children's television programming that seeks to keep kids attentive so they'll watch the commercials, our ministries of diversion respond to young people's most carnal appetites so that we can slip in a five-minute Bible study or parade them through the church building.

Ministry programmes that respond to the anxiety of adults and/or youth are incapable of awakening kids to the freedom of God. Rather than trusting the presence of God, these reactive ministries put their faith in attendance, conversions and confirmation class sizes. To get these results and to assuage fears, they become more and more about control and manipulation. Kids know, even when they can't articulate it, when a ministry is concerned with control and manipulation. They know when the purpose of the ministry is to alleviate fear. They know when ministries are simply about protecting young people from the realities of life.

Once young people recognize that youth ministry is really about quelling anxiety, one of two things can happen. If the ministry is uninteresting or provides few social opportunities, the young people will eventually leave. If the ministry provides youth with fun outings and occasions to socialize with friends, the young people are happy to play along – provided the ministry is entertaining, the youth are happy to ease the fears of the congregation. They assent to being paraded in front of congregations ('Don't worry, the church isn't dying!'); doted over by congregational leaders ('No fear! Your financial allocations are producing results!'); photographed for the church newsletter ('Have no doubts, Christianity is alive and well!'). As long as there are trips to Disneyland, church dances and the annual summer mission trip, they're happy to pretend. Just don't expect them to be around once they leave high school – or when the programme budget dries up. Then they'll have to get on with the real stuff of life.

2

Life without expectations

Religion is not our concern; it is God's concern. The sooner we stop thinking we are the energetic operators of religion and discover that God is at work . . . so much the sooner do we discover that our task is to call people *to be still and know*, listen, hearken in quiet invitation to the subtle promptings of the Divine. Our task is to encourage others first to let go, to cease striving, to give over this fevered effort of the self-sufficient religionist trying to please an external deity. I am persuaded that religious people do not with sufficient seriousness count on God as an active factor in the affairs of the world. 'Behold, I stand at the door and knock', but too many well-intentioned people are so preoccupied with the clatter of effort to do something for God that they don't hear Him asking that He might do something *through* them.

(Thomas Kelly, *A Testament of Devotion*)

You don't have to fix things. God is already there. You just have to be open to God's love and transparent to what God is doing.

(Alexx Campbell, age 18, San Anselmo, California)

The anxieties present in youth ministry are not an abstraction to me.

I was 25 years old, newly married, and in my first full-time job as a youth pastor at a mid-sized Presbyterian church in Portland, Oregon. The congregation had just completed a 12-year campaign to build a new youth facility with a large multi-purpose room and two youth classrooms.

Although this was my first paid job in youth ministry, I felt experienced and well trained. My father, Mike Yaconelli (considered one of the founders of youth ministry in North America) was the owner of Youth Specialties, a company that produced workshops, conventions and publications to train youth ministers. I had attended these events since I was a toddler, and had spent countless hours among teens and highly capable youth ministers. I had a library filled with the latest curricula, exercises and models for sharing the Christian faith with young people.

So it was a surprise when, after two-and-a-half years in the ministry, I realized I was a failure. The signs were obvious. When I was hired, there were approximately ten teenagers involved in worship and Sunday school. At that time the church leadership gave me a list of almost 50 teens from church families who were uninvolved in church activities. In my first few months at the church, many of these families had me over for dinner or met me after worship and introduced me to their children. The expectation was clear: I was to find a way to get these kids involved in the church and form them in the Christian faith. Yet despite doubling the number of youth events, increasing the youth budget and working 70 hours a week, the youth programme appeared stagnant under my leadership. It seemed the only kids interested in church or the Christian faith were the ten who were already involved when I arrived – and sometimes even they didn't show up.

Parents and other church members began to express frustration that I wasn't attracting more youth to the church. Most of the young people within the congregation seemed to be avoiding me. I was called in to talk to the personnel committee who asked for a better description of how I spent my time. Other youth directors in the area expressed surprise when I showed up to regional gatherings with only two or three kids. 'Aren't you Mike Yaconelli's son?' they would ask. 'Where's the rest of your youth group?'

Each week there was a public ritual that highlighted my failure as a youth pastor. In order to encourage more young people to attend Sunday morning services, the Christian education committee had created a 'youth pew' where young people were invited to sit together during worship. Of course, the youth pew was in the very front row, visible to the entire congregation. Each week I was expected to sit with the youth as the designated host and chaperone. I began to dread Sunday mornings. I would wait until the last possible moment and then, while the congregation was standing and singing, I would slink up the side aisle and take my assigned seat. I often sat nervously perspiring, waiting to see if some teenager would join me. In reality, I wasn't sure what to hope for. To be alone in the youth pew was a public sign that kids didn't want to hang out with me; on the other hand, to sit helpless while two or three uninterested kids slept, punched holes in the church bulletin, or removed the stick pins from the designated visitor ribbons and pierced their palms like Cheyenne warriors was a painful sign of my ineffectiveness.

I began to suffer more and more anxiety. I felt like a fool, embarrassed to admit the job was too much for me. I wanted desperately for the kids to like me. I wanted to meet the expectations of the church leadership. I wanted to create a bold group of teenage Jesus-lovers. I wanted to quell the frustration of tithing parents. I wanted to live up to my dad's reputation. I wanted to fulfil my own images of success.

Instead, I suffered insomnia. I couldn't sleep more than a few hours a night. My wife hardly saw me. I tried to burn my anxiety by putting in more hours. I would leave home at seven in the morning to drive the school bus routes, offering kids rides; then I'd spend evenings attending high-school sporting events or phoning various teens to try to coax them to attend Sunday school. I spent weekends helping out at other Christian youth programmes – hoping their kids might come over to our church. I volunteered in schools across town and spent afternoons handing out hot chocolate at bus stops. But nothing seemed to work.

I even tried to bribe kids. I provided doughnuts and caffe lattes at morning Sunday school, and cookies and soda at each youth meeting. I picked kids up during the school lunch break and took them out to their favourite fast-food hang-outs. The young people seemed wary and unresponsive – they liked the treats but expressed no interest in the Christian life or the church. No matter how many young people I contacted during the week, the same ten kids showed up for every Sunday school class or youth event. I finally fell into a depression when it occurred to me that the kids who were participating didn't care about the time and effort I was putting into the programme. They just liked being together – and planned to show up whether I was there or not.

When my wife expressed concern about my long work hours and nights away from home, I responded with irritation: Didn't she realize I was doing God's work? Wasn't it clear I was seeking to save the souls of the young people within the community? Couldn't she see I was failing? Didn't she realize I was going to have to work harder to share the good news? Didn't she remember that Jesus was killed doing the very same thing? Wasn't it obvious I was going to have to suffer trials and tribulations in order to get these overscheduled, middle-class teenagers to see the significance of the Christian life?

Of course, underneath my anger and frustration was a sickening suspicion that my ministry to teenagers was stagnant because *my* faith was weak. I committed myself to becoming a more effective Christian. I bought a devotional book and spent an additional hour each morning in prayer and Bible study. I prayed for each kid in the church by name, pleading with God to increase the number of youth in the programme – or at least motivate some kids to become followers of Jesus. Surely these acts of devotion would convince God to bring me success!

Instead, the numbers dropped. Soon I had only a handful of kids attending Sunday school and youth group programmes. I began to suffer dizzy spells. The low point arrived when only one kid signed up for our annual summer camp – a camp I'd spent hundreds of hours planning and organizing with four other churches. I began to feel there was nothing I could do to please God, the young people, or the church. I became resentful. I began to tell myself that the Christian life was too heavy and burdensome and I was not cut out to do ministry. I became withdrawn from my wife and friends.

Looking back, it's easy to see that this whirlwind of effort wasn't really about the Christian life. Although I believed I was trying to help young people discover Jesus' way of love, in reality I was more worried about meeting expectations. It seemed my driving concern was to please kids, please parents, please the church, and please God. I desperately wanted to meet these exterior expectations so I would know I was worth something; so I could mitigate my inner fears that I was a failure as a disciple and human being. The ministry was just a means through which I was seeking tangible proof that I was loved by God – or at least by young people. Thus, the focus of my ministry wasn't God's love, but rather the anxiety and expectations of myself and the other adults in the church. And the kids could smell it.

Sadly, this kind of anxiety is a common motivator within Western Christianity, often masking itself as spiritual passion. I recognize this same anxiety to succeed among many pastors, parents and Christian outreach programmes directed at youth. It's a driven-ness to perform, an obsession with results, a concentration on goals and outcomes that discounts the ordinary graces and small cries for mercy inhabiting our daily lives. Deeper than that, such driven ministries point to a God who appears as a distant ideal or set of principles, a stern moralizer full of demands and expectations. Our anxiety-filled ministries expose an unspoken belief that God is utterly untrustworthy, that God's impotence has forced us to take responsibility for the souls of young people ourselves.

Of course, this is in complete contrast to the patient trust and downward mobility of Jesus. Unlike the efficiency experts populating Western Christianity, Jesus wasn't focused on abstract goals and principles. Jesus seemed to be a person deeply concerned with the small picture. He seemed content to receive the people and situations directly in front of him. He seemed satisfied that trusting God and others in the present moment was enough to communicate the reality of God's life. Jesus' ministry lacks anxiety – despite the fears of the disciples, the incredible needs of people, and the vindictive anger of those in power.

Fortunately for me there was an associate pastor at the church I served in who was seeking to carry the same trust that Jesus embodied. Through regular meetings and conversation, we developed a friendship, and I learned to trust his insight. One day he invited me to attend a retreat led by an Episcopal priest and author, Morton Kelsey. I was reluctant to attend – it seemed an inefficient use of my time when I had hundreds of young people to save. I bowed out, blaming the high retreat fee and my lack of transportation. But my friend knew I needed some time away and, without my knowledge, applied for a scholarship on my behalf. One week later he informed me that my fee had been paid, and he would drive me to the convent each day so I could attend the sessions. I was out of excuses and reluctantly agreed to go along.

The conference was held at the Franciscan Renewal Center, a former convent that the few remaining sisters had refurbished and were operating as a retreat centre. The first session was on a Monday night. As soon as we entered the room, I wished I hadn't come. It was a small, pastel-tiled gymnasium. The walls were partially covered in pock-marked, sound-proofing tile, much of which was dissolving into tired brown cardboard. On one side of the room were 40 or 50 metal chairs set out on various coloured carpet pieces. Grey partitions were placed along the back row to create a makeshift enclosure. After appraising the setting, I scanned the participants. It was my most feared combo: white-haired ladies and overly-friendly pastor types peppered with wall-flowers, loners and introverts scribbling in bloated notebooks. Except for one woman in her late twenties, I was the youngest person there by 25 years.

We took our seats, and one of the sisters came forward to lead us in a song. It was immediately awkward. Without instruments to guide us, the melody was elusive. Half the group remained silent while the other half overcompensated with voices that could have exorcised the Christian faith from Mother Teresa. I stood and quietly mouthed along while the ageing sister sang. For the rest of the week she began each session in the same way. I still remember the words:

> Open our eyes, Lord,
> Help us to see your face.
> Open our eyes, Lord,
> Help us to see.

Open our ears, Lord,
Help us to hear your voice.
Open our ears, Lord,
Help us to hear.

Open our hearts, Lord,
Help us to love like you.
Open our hearts, Lord,
Help us to love.

I live within you,
Deep in your heart, O Love.
I live within you,
Rest now in me.

After we sat down our host offered some staff introductions, explained the schedule, and introduced the retreat speaker. Seventy-year-old Morton Kelsey reminded me at first of the scarecrow in *The Wizard of Oz*. He was tall, gangly and presented a long, narrow face grooved with smile lines. He wore a plaid western shirt with a bolo tie and wobbled when he walked, like a man stepping off a freighter after a season at sea. Thick black-rimmed glasses held his eyes, and bulging flesh-coloured hearing aids hung on each ear. Morton took his time making his way to the front, steadied himself, then panned the room with such a broad goofy grin that I was certain he'd wandered away from a nearby nursing home.

When Morton spoke, his voice was gentle, slow and sing-songy. Words were rounded like the speech of the partially deaf. Somehow this was comforting and less intimidating. At times he would say something that would strike him funny, causing a great gasping sort of laugh that set us all off-guard. Other times he spoke of his encounters with suffering with such stillness that you could feel the emptiness within him. I remember listening to him speak that first night as if the world were enchanted and infused with the possibility and presence of God.

That night and each subsequent morning Morton gave a meditation on a parable. Most of them were from Luke 15 (the lost coin, the lost sheep, the prodigal son). He spoke of the spiritual reality these parables revealed – a reality of love and mercy that he claimed was more real than the limited win/lose world of consumption that most of us inhabited. Although his ideas were illuminating, it was the place from which his words arose that I found most striking. Morton seemed to speak from the inside. There was a knowing, an experience of God, that carried his words to the door of the heart. Although he was highly educated, when he spoke of God's love it wasn't out of study or prescribed doctrine. He seemed to speak from something he'd seen with his own eyes, heard with his own (broken) ears, touched with his own hands, and felt with his own heart. I began to sense that for Morton, God was not a moral principle or a heroic ideal, but rather a very ordinary and living presence – a presence that, through the life of Jesus, seemed to be offering a boundless, shameless kind of love within each and every moment.

After each talk Morton invited us to engage in some sort of spiritual exercise. Throughout my upbringing as a Christian I had engaged in numerous 'faith-building' exercises. Most were educational drills that relied on study and discussion to help assimilate spiritual or religious information. Yet the exercises Morton prescribed were different, for they were primarily invitations to *encounter* God. Rather than words, study and reason, they relied on silence, prayer and imagination. I later discovered that many of these exercises are part of the ancient and forgotten contemplative prayer tradition within the Christian Church. Rather than treat God as a means to an end, these disciplines and exercises invited one to 'be' with God, to move inside and seek the presence of God without expectation. This was new to me, and in direct contrast to a Christian upbringing that, until then, was focused on words, moral principles and good works. It had never occurred to me to actually seek to be with God, to open myself to God without an end in mind.

On the third day of the retreat, we were asked to imagine ourselves within the story of the prodigal son – allowing ourselves to see, hear and feel the events of the story as if we were present. The group dispersed, and each person was to find a quiet, solitary place in which to pray. Immediately I went to my friend and asked

if we could leave early. He was a little surprised, and then told me
he had committed to helping the staff that day and couldn't take
me home. He asked if I was going to do the prayer exercise. I
replied that I understood the basic meaning of the exercise and
didn't feel the need to waste time doing it. He shrugged his shoulders, mumbled, 'Well, I think I'll give it a try', and walked off.

Feeling a little admonished, I resigned myself to enter the
prayer. I walked down into the basement of the building and
found a small prayer chapel. I set out my Bible, read the parable,
and then closed my eyes and waited, allowing the story to take
place within me from beginning to end. At one point in the
silence, I felt a tangible and disarming sense of welcome. It was an
overwhelming reality of love and acceptance that poured into
each of my senses, leaving me shaking with tears and filled with a
deep sense of rest.

When I got control of myself, I exited the room, certain I was
experiencing some sort of psychological breakdown. The experience had been so ultra-real that I suspected the months of anxiety
about my ministry and faith-life had finally split me open. I knew
Morton was trained in psychotherapy, so I approached him
quietly at the end of our next gathering and asked if I could speak
with him alone. That night after dinner we skipped evening
vespers and found a small classroom away from the group. I told
him about my experience in prayer – the sense of love and acceptance, the outpouring of tears, and the deep sense of relief. I also
told him of my months of anxiety and asked him if I was having
a nervous breakdown. Gently, he asked questions about my family
life, my work situation and my upbringing. With each story I
shared, he would respond by telling pieces of his own life history
– often sharing experiences similar to my own. I soon noticed
how calm I felt as we discovered similarities in our relationships
with our fathers and our work within the Church.

After a couple of hours, we were winding down. Morton rose
and put on his jacket. I panicked for a moment, realizing my
question hadn't been answered. I blurted out, 'So am I having a
breakdown or not?'

Morton paused, smiled at me, and then said, 'Well, what do you
think? You seem calm, comfortable and open. Do those seem like

the signs of someone having a breakdown?' I had to admit I was feeling a sense of rest and relief that was new and attractive. He said, 'Mark, my guess is you had some encounter with God's love, and maybe now you can believe God has no expectations of you.'

I tried to let this sink in. We walked to the door and Morton gave me his phone number and address. He told me he'd be available any time I wanted to talk, day or night. 'But,' he said, 'only call if you want to.' I nodded my head. He looked at me again and said, 'It's up to you. If you wish to talk more, I would be delighted to carry on our conversation. But if I don't hear from you, I will be glad we had this time and won't be upset or worried in any way.' I nodded a second time and started to thank him for the time. He gently grabbed my arm to stop me and said a third time, 'You understand that if you contact me, I will be happy to talk. But I will be equally satisfied if you never contact me again.'

Finally, it struck me what he was trying to communicate. My throat tightened. He then said, 'You see, I'm trying to tell you I have no expectations of you. Just as God has no expectations of you. God offers love to you, just as you are. I have enjoyed our conversation and I am open to whatever happens after this. It's up to you.' I looked down and nodded, my eyes heavy with tears.

Three days later I entered the junior-high youth room at the Presbyterian church I served filled with a new source of energy. I had come in contact with the reality of God's presence in the world – and this changed everything. It was as if the scales had dropped from my eyes. Suddenly I was filled with questions: If God is alive and present, then how is God moving within the ministry? If God is so available, then how is God present to each of these kids?

Almost overnight, the ministry no longer seemed to rely on me and my skills. It no longer seemed to be about my anxious attempts to attract kids or conjure up God. Instead, I realized my role was secondary. I realized God is the deep reality of life, not just a hope or ideal. God is alive and actively seeking to invite each of these young people into a relationship of love. My role was to get out of the centre, to let God do the ministering, to act as a midwife, helping young people notice and name God's presence within their daily lives.

It occurred to me then that the failure or success of the ministry had never been in my hands. Suddenly I felt I could relax. I could release my tight hold on the outcomes of the ministry and instead seek simply to be faithful, open and present to God and the young people. Strangely, this seemed to be similar to the way Jesus shared his faith. Open and available. Present and trusting. Patient and waiting, confident he didn't need to control or manipulate anyone. Trusting that his presence – his prayers, words, silences and acts of love – would be enough.

3

Staying alive

The adults who make Christianity come alive are the adults who take an interest in me – the adults who show an interest in my life as well as a passion and interest in their own lives. Not only do they say, 'Hey, how are things going with you?' They're also willing to sit down and say, 'Let me tell you what's going on with me.' Those are the people I really enjoy. Those are the people who have kept me in church.

(Nathaniel, age 19, Eugene, Oregon)

The glory of God is manifest in the person fully alive.

(Irenaeus of Lyon)

One of the primary pressures we face in youth ministry is to make kids nice. In a recent survey parents were asked their most important goal in raising children. The most common response was, 'To raise a moral person'. In order to attain this goal, many parents bring their children to church.

What is the desire for 'good kids' about? It means adults don't want kids to get into trouble. Parents want them to be safe from bad kids and bad deeds. Church members want youth who are courteous and respectful. Adults want youth to do as they say and not cause problems. Parents want youth to make them proud and avoid embarrassing misbehaviour. If I were to put into words the most immediate, surface question many parents have when they bring their kids to church, it would be this: 'Can you help me keep my child safe and good?'

I was invited to a meeting at a local church to talk about youth ministry. Parents and other church members were distressed that young people had stopped attending, despite the church's investing time and money in an activity-packed youth programme called Youth Power! Instead of discussing the specifics of the youth programme, I asked people to tell me why they wanted kids in church. People were startled at first and looked at me as if the answer were obvious. Then they began to respond. One man called out, 'Church is good for kids.'

'Can you be more specific?' I asked.

'Church is where kids learn values and morals,' he responded.

Then a mother spoke up, 'I want my kids involved in the church so they can get involved in something positive. I don't want them getting into trouble or hanging out with bad kids.'

Most of the remaining comments were along these lines. I stopped the discussion and said, 'I have a recommendation. If your primary reason for wanting young people in church is to keep them moral and protected, then you should be upfront and tell them. I suggest you change the name of the youth group from Youth Power! to Nice and Safe!' They laughed, knowing none of their kids would be interested in a programme that sounded so bland and protective.

There was a pause, then one father spoke up, 'You know, I bet the reason our kids don't like coming to church is because they know it's all about us. They know that despite all the outings and activities the programme is really about our desire to teach them to stay out of trouble.' As this insight began to fill the room, many of the adults felt embarrassed at the exposure of their real intentions.

I reminded the group that it's good to want our kids to be protected and moral. I asked them, however, to take a moment and notice if there weren't a deeper desire they harboured for their children and the other young people of the church. I gave them a period of silence, urging them to simply rest for a while and then turn a simple awareness toward the depths of their heart. I then asked them to see if they noticed words that helped express their deepest hope for young people.

The silence was rich and full. Some people welled up with tears. After a few minutes I asked people to share what they'd noticed. Here are some of the responses I collected:

- My hope is that my daughter will know how much she's loved.
- I hope our young people can have a sense of God's joy and peace even in hard times.
- I want our young people to know they have a community of faith that will carry them.
- My hope is that our young people will live lives of love.
- I hope my children will know God is as close as their heartbeat, offering strength and comfort when they need it.
- I hope our kids will see Jesus as a friend, and realize they're not alone.
- My hope is that our young people will know they are not just consumers, or statistics, or employees – that they have gifts and abilities God has given them. I want them to know they're uniquely made by God.
- I want our kids to know they belong to a long history of people who have followed Jesus in standing up to injustice and bringing light into the world.
- My hope is that our young people will have a faith that will help them know when the culture is trying to use or exploit them.

Take a moment to set down this book and prayerfully reflect on your own hope for young people. Gently and silently become aware of God's presence, then simply ask, 'What is my deepest hope for the young people I know?' Then wait. Don't force anything. Just see what words and images arise.

*   *   *

The Bible says people brought their kids to Jesus 'to have him touch them' (Mark 10.13; Luke 18.15). I believe this same desire exists in the heart of parents and congregations today. We want our kids to be touched. We want them to be blessed. We want them to make contact with the Source of life. We want them to know the freedom of Jesus. We want them to be alive as spiritual beings, despite the consequences and dangers of our materialistic culture.

As I touch into my own hope for my children and the youth I minister with, I am overcome with an overwhelming sense of gratitude. It's as if this hope is not mine, but rather something that has been given to me. The anxiety around my kids and ministry diminishes, and I am left with a paradoxical sense of deep yearning and deep satisfaction. I often ask workshop participants, once they have identified their primary hope for young people, to spend time in silent prayer asking God to make them aware of God's hope for young people. When I ask for responses, people generally notice that God's hope for their children is the same or similar to their own. There's a surprising awareness that their hope for young people is not something they created or made up. It is God's hope. It is a gift, given to them to carry, to follow, to live into by faith. 'We hope for what we do not see,' Paul says to the Romans (8.25).

We have no clear plan for how to actuate this hope. We simply hold our hope for our kids. Hoping for things that seem unattainable – hoping for things we know not how to provide. And yet all the anxieties and fears around our young people seem to dissipate in the face of our unquenchable hope.

What is our hope for young people? We want them to live. We want them to be alive. We want them to be free. We want them to experience Jesus, because we know, somewhere deep within us, that only God can keep them alive. We know it's possible to grow old without having lived. We know you can become so busy accumulating stuff, so distracted by the marketplace, so comfortable and insulated by technologies, that you can miss your life.

Beneath adult anxiety about young people is a real and persistent hope that young people will become fully alive and open to love. Parents want their kids to live, to thrive, to experience joy, to create lives rich in relationship and possibility. It turns out that this same hope undergirds teenage anxiety about adults. Beneath adolescent anxieties about adults are more profound longings to experience lives that are passionate, meaningful and full of deep connection to others. In fact, if I had to sum up the primary question young people seem to be asking within every interaction with adults, it would be this: 'Do you know how to stay alive?'

Do you know how to stay alive? Beneath the anxiety, youth want to know how to live fully in this world. They are asking us: Do you know how to become yourself despite the constant messages telling you that you're lacking? Do you know how to keep from becoming overwhelmed by the pain and suffering in the world? Do you know how to find a home, a place of welcome and relationship? Can you tell me how to stay hopeful and creative despite a world obsessed with violence, death and conformity? Do you know where I can offer my gifts meaningfully within a world that feels consumed with trivia? How do I stay alive? How do I remain open to God and others when so many people seem closed, distant and angry?'

This list of questions may seem overwhelming – rarely do youth ask these questions so blatantly. More often they come embedded in questions concerning career choices. It's what they're listening for when they ask about our own decision processes and learn how we made the transition to adulthood. Youth want to know why we believe in God. They want to know about our marriages or romantic lives. They want to meet our friends and find out what we do when we're not in church. They want to know what makes us angry and whether we agree or disagree with their parents. Beneath these questions is a hunger to know how to live well, how to avoid the despair and sullenness that seem to possess many adults.

I believe our attempts to share the Christian life with young people must continually be measured according to how we respond to this question of becoming fully alive. The truth is that most of us who seek to share Jesus' life with young people are not great programme administrators, entertainers, psychotherapists or family counsellors. We're not particularly skilled at designing exciting, educational curricula. No, the real gift we have to offer young people is this: we yearn to become fully alive. We long to live lives of deep connection. We struggle to resist our own damning, self-protective habits. We seek to live more honest and authentic lives despite a world fixated on pretending. We stretch toward God, the source of love, amidst the cynicism, materialism and despair. 'God is not the God of the dead but of the living', and as lovers of God, we want to be animated by that same life (Matthew 22.32).

If we take the yearnings of young people seriously, then we can admit to ourselves that young people aren't interested in our answers (often given in response to questions they're not asking). They're not looking for alternative, safe activities. What they're seeking is the companionship of adults who embody a different way of *being*. They're looking for living adults who have room inside them. Room for creativity and compassion, room to hold the suffering and ambiguities of life, room to listen and reflect on the hard questions, room to see the larger wholeness that exists beneath our fragmented societies. Young people are looking for adults who can guide them toward a different way of being, of living in the world. They are looking for adults who know how to live lives of love.

Ultimately as Christians, we trust that Jesus really is about becoming fully alive. We believe Jesus when he says, 'I came that you may have life, and have it abundantly' (John 10.10). This is what Christians offer young people. Becoming alive is the Way of Jesus. This is the heart of our desire to share the Christian life with young people. This is the deeper purpose beneath our attempts to teach and model a moral life. This is why we want youth in worship. This is why we want to expose them to a Christian community. This is what motivates our youth programmes and Sunday school classes.

Can we trust that our longing to become fully alive is a powerful gift to young people? Can we take heart that our desire for God will be enough?

4

Becoming a good receiver

You will discover that the more love you can take in and hold on to, the less fearful you will become. You will speak more simply, more directly and more freely about what is important to you, without fear of other people's reactions. You will also use fewer words, trusting that you communicate your true self even when you do not speak much. The more you come to know yourself – spirit, mind and body – as truly loved, the freer you will be to proclaim the good news. That is the freedom of the children of God.

(Henri Nouwen, *The Inner Voice of Love*)

I receive a thank-you note from a seventh-grader named Alex. After a year, two brothers begin to open up about their painful home life. A young high-schooler tells me the truth about his sexuality. An older church member sends me an e-mail that he's begun to notice our young people on Sunday mornings. It occurs to me that if I was only concerned with 'teaching' these kids, instead of listening and receiving, I would have missed these gems.

(Leanna Creel, film-maker, youth ministry volunteer, Immanuel Presbyterian Church, Los Angeles, California)

For Jesus, becoming alive means becoming open and available to God's love. Jesus invites us to trust that underneath our anxious striving, beneath our worry and life-management strategies there is the reality of God's love. I use the word *reality* because too often within the Church 'God's love' refers to some future ideal, ecclesial principle or sentimental hope. But this would be a misunderstand-ing of Jesus' life. Jesus lives his life as if there is a boundless, shame-less love present and available within every moment. He lives his life rooted in an unseen world more spacious and forgiving than the harried world that most of us inhabit. Jesus seems to live a life that is 'rooted and grounded in love'. Within the reality of God's love, people and situations appear different to Jesus; his eyes and ears notice things that others seem unable to perceive. Through the presence of God's love, Jesus is able to feel and respond to the inner truth of each situation.

For Jesus, God's love and presence is tangible, intimate and knowable. God's love is the source of our being and the endpoint of our deepest yearnings. Through his words and actions Jesus communicates that this Presence of love can be trusted. Jesus seems to gently nudge us over and over to see, hear and touch this love for ourselves. He wants us to open our eyes and ears and see that God isn't an abstract belief; God is a present reality, available and trustworthy, offering us rest and inspiration. He tells us that the key to becoming fully free and alive is to *participate* in God's love: 'Love God with all your heart, mind, soul and body; and love your neighbour as you love yourself.'

For most of us this is not a new idea. We know that we yearn for God's love. We know that young people seek to receive and share God's love. And yet, we're not very good at loving. Most of us have had poor family and church models of what it means to love. And so the question still remains: How do we open to a life of love in the midst of an overly busy, over-stimulated, callous and preoccupied society? How do we participate authentically in God's love in the midst of buzzing and blooming teenagers? Further, how do we help young people become aware of this love within their own lives?

One thing is clear: we can't create love. We can't conjure up God's love by offering kids sugary smiles and inspirational posters. Even if we seek to serve kids – help them with homework, drive them to and from school – even these good acts can be heavy and oppressive to young people if they don't come from love. We can't create more love for ourselves or our kids, because the truth is that love can not be *made*, it can only be *received*. Love is a gift that God offers to us, a gift that asks only that we let down our resistances and yield.

Surrender

If love is a gift, then to live a life of love the first thing we need to do is to surrender. We need to stop seeking to make kids love God (or make God love our kids). To carry the Good News is to trust that God's love is present and available to our young people even when our youth programmes and ministries are neurotic, self-absorbed disasters. To share the Christian life with young people means to let God be God, and trust that our desire to share faith with young people will be enough. To surrender means to recognize that we don't control God. We don't control how God lives and moves. We don't control our churches, and we certainly don't control the spiritual lives of our young people. If Paul is to be believed in the New Testament than we can assert that we don't even control ourselves! 'I do not understand my own actions. For I do not do what I want, but I do the very thing I hate' (Romans 7.15).

Once we can admit our own powerlessness to turn kids into Christians, perhaps then we can realize that ministry is a series of small acts of trust. It's more about yielding to what is already present and available than about creating or building. It's more about an attitude of trust than a mind catalogued with belief statements. If we can see that we're not in control of our ministries, maybe we can hear the truth that Mother Teresa once articulated – that in our ministries we're 'not seeking to be successful but merely faithful'. The end results of our labours are in God's hands. Hopefully we can trust that our young people belong to God. That God has been seeking to love our young people since before they were born and will continue to love them long after they leave the influence of our ministries.

I have observed too many churches and youth ministries whose methods are in direct contrast to their belief statements, exposing a consistent distrust of God. These ministries embody a sense of urgency that communicates a God who is either a relentless taskmaster or completely incompetent. This is the 'functional atheism' of which Parker Palmer writes. In youth ministry this is the endless parade of duded-up Christian rock stars, hyperactive activities, word-heavy programmes, and teen devotionals covered in exclamation marks!!!!! There is a tangible sense that God must be dressed up or hidden behind high-energy music and charismatic speakers. Our churches and ministries seem to be deathly afraid of any kind of downtime. All silence and stillness is eradicated for fear that young people might find God disappointing, boring or absent. It's as if our church and ministry leaders have an anxious suspicion that God has left the building, and so they stall with jabbering words and meaningless activities in the hope the crowd won't become restless.

In contrast, Jesus isn't afraid of doubts, or downtime, or disappointment or boredom – in fact, I might even claim that he finds boredom, disappointment and doubt critical to spiritual growth! He's not embarrassed or ashamed of God's presence – even when God appears ineffective in the face of great evil and suffering. Jesus wants us to make contact with our real situations in life. He loves the true, living, mysterious reality of God more than our names and images of God. He trusts that if we seek the truth of our existence, we will discover the reality of God's abundant love. And so Jesus asks us to stop. He invites us to come away to quiet and deserted places. He asks us to *be still and know.* He calls us to take a moment to do nothing. He calls us to turn our attention away from our anxiety and busyness and just simply notice the work that God is already doing.

When my wife was pregnant with our first child she noticed that when she was actively running errands and doing chores around the house she rarely felt the baby move. It was only when she stopped, sat still or lay down that she could feel the baby's activity. Sometimes at night I would have these private moments with my unborn child. I would wait until Jill fell asleep, then I would reach over and place my hand on her stomach. I would lie there, feeling the baby shifting and moving. I would sit in wonder at this growing person stirring inside. It's the same with us. Unless we regularly stop the activity and sit still for a moment, we often miss making contact with the life waiting to be born. We miss God's Spirit moving within and around us.

When we stop all of our activity we discover what is really driving our lives. To stop and surrender is to repent. It is to turn away from our preoccupations and remember the One who has gone before us. When we stay still for a moment we become aware of the source of our activity, we begin to see what propels our ministries and relationships with young people. In stopping we can awaken to the real source of our faith – whether it be our own anxious fear or our hunger for God's love. And when we stop and stay still we become available to receive the gift of love that God has been waiting to give us.

Receive

To live into God's love and create ministries that offer young people Jesus' way of life, we not only have to stop, we have to also be willing to receive. The Christian life begins by receiving. We don't know much about receiving in the West. For most of us, life is what you make of it. 'What do you do?' (or for young people, 'What are you going to do?') is the first question we ask someone and for too many of us our response to this question becomes the basis of our identity. To live, in the West, is to do; and unfortunately the imagined purpose of life both within and outside of the Christian Church is to become efficient and productive. Life is measured by the success of our own individual efforts and ingenuity.

In contrast, a life of love is open-ended. Love isn't in a hurry to get somewhere, it doesn't live for the end result. Love takes pleasure in the here and now. Love seeks relationships. Love is not a means to an end. Love is its own reward. Paul writes that love is patient, kind, bears all things, hopes all things, endures all things (1 Corinthians 13.4–7). If God is love (1 John), then we can add that these are not only descriptions of love, but also descriptions of the God who is alive and working within every moment.

Jesus is the best teacher for how we might live a life of love amidst young people. Perhaps the most significant difference between Jesus and other people is that Jesus is a good receiver. He receives food from the cheating tax-collector. He allows a prostitute to pour expensive oil on his feet. He lets children embrace him and people shout his praises. Most importantly, Jesus is also willing to receive from God. When Jesus comes to the Jordan river to be baptized, the Scriptures tell us that he heard a voice from God that said, 'You are my son, the Beloved, with you I am well pleased.' Now, many of us who have been Christians have heard many times that God loves us and cherishes us as God's beloved – yet how many of us really believe this? How many of us slow down and take the time for this experience of love to penetrate the depths of our being? How many of us have faith that God only loves our good deeds, our self-sacrifices, our moments of prayer or devotion? How many of us are convinced that God's love reaches us only when we say the right words and walk within the right lines? How many of us are driven by an unsettling anxiety that the Christian life is something one earns or achieves? It may be that the essential difference between Jesus and others is that when he hears God call him 'Beloved' he doesn't question it: he simply believes it. He receives God's name of love before he has done any great works – before he has performed healings, before speaking insights, before undergoing any sacrifices.

Jesus fully accepts that he is the beloved of God before he has begun his public ministry. He accepts, fully, that he is loved. And this makes all the difference. Having received this love from God, he is able to tolerate the doubts, false accusations, curses and even hatred poured out at him – because deep within his heart he knows and trusts the love that God offers him. He knows within the marrow of his bones that he is beloved by God, and that this is the deeper truth of his identity. Who would we be if we lived with the same knowledge? How would we interact with young people if we claimed our belovedness in God?

When we allow ourselves to be open and receptive to God's love and presence, we suddenly begin to notice that God is alive and available. We begin to perceive that the Holy Spirit has been present and working beneath the worry and activity of our ministries. It may even occur to us that God has been present to our young people long before we entered the ministry. Our ministries are transformed as we trust in the knowledge that God has been ministering to our young people since before they were created in their mother's womb, and long before they met us. When we stop to receive God's life and love, we begin to understand that the Holy Spirit has been seeking our young people with greater passion and desire than we could ever work up. In our amazement at the ministry God is doing, it becomes clear to us that our ministry is really not about us. We notice a sense of relief that we're not the centre of the ministry. We discover new-found energy as it dawns on us that our role in youth ministry is not to 'make something happen'! Our task is simply to be in wonder at what God is doing, and then to lend a hand as we're needed.

5

Allowing God to love us

My quiet time is the only place where I can just sigh, and let my shoulders drop. I've come to a point in my prayer life that I no longer need to say anything to God or perform a certain prayer. I can just sit there and know my intention to be in prayer is enough.

When I first started hanging out with youth I felt I had to ask them a lot of questions, make jokes and make them feel good. Now I plop down next to them and sigh and ask, 'How are you?' Whether their response is a word or a five-minute monologue, I can sit with them knowing that my attention to them for that five seconds or five minutes is enough.

When I look back on my prayer life with God, I can't remember what we've said to each other, but I know that God has been around all my life. When I recall the adults in my life who have shown me love, I don't remember anything they've ever said to me. I just remember that when we were together one way or another they paid attention to me. Those memories of God and adults sustain me even to this day.

(Adam Yoder, youth pastor, Seattle Mennonite Church,
Seattle, Washington)

Perfect love casts out fear.

(1 John 4.18)

Changing the way in which we relate to young people isn't just a matter of developing new techniques or broadening our theology. It's about a different attitude of the heart. It's about being present to young people with a loving transparency. We're seeking to see teens with the eyes of Jesus, hear teens with the ears of Jesus, and perceive teens with the heart of Jesus.

Below is a very simple description of the different ways in which we go about ministry when we're rooted in anxiety versus love. Notice the qualitative difference between a life and ministry based on patience and love, as opposed to one fuelled by fear and anxiety. Although our ministries and actions are never this clearly defined, the following descriptions of these two dispositions point toward the kind of transformation we seek to undergo as ministers.

Anxiety seeks **control** (How do I make kids into Christians?)	*Love seeks **contemplation** (How can I be present to kids and God?)*
Anxiety seeks **professionals** (Who is the expert that can solve the youth problem?)	*Love seeks **processes** (What can we do together to uncover Jesus' way of life?)*
Anxiety wants **products** (What book, video, curriculum will teach kids faith?)	*Love desires **presence** (Who will bear the life of God among teenagers?)*
Anxiety lifts up **gurus** (Who has the charisma to draw kids?)	*Love relies on **guides** (Who has the gifts for living alongside kids?)*
Anxiety rests in **results** (How many kids have committed to the faith?)	*Love rests in **relationships** (Who are the kids we've befriended?)*
Anxiety seeks **conformity** (Are the young people meeting our expectations?)	*Love brings out **creativity** (What's the fresh way in which God is challenging us through our youth?)*
Anxiety wants **activity** (What will keep the kids busy?)	*Love brings **awareness** (What are the real needs of the youth?)*
Anxiety seeks **answers** (Here's what we think. Here's who God is.)	*Love seeks **questions** (What do you think? Or as Jesus said, 'Who do you say that I am?')*

We cannot undergo this transformation by the sheer strength of our own will or intellect. It's only by yielding that we can even begin to embody the freedom of God. We have to let go and allow God to transform our anxiety into love; to allow God to show us a new way of being in the world, a new way of engaging in relationships with young people; to allow the Holy Spirit to teach us how to live from the heart rather than the head. We have to allow God to 'de-programme' us from habitually relating to kids as projects that need managing rather than persons who need God's love and trust.

If we are to awaken young people to the reality of God's love, we need moments of open, receptive prayer. When we slow down and feel the life of Jesus in Scripture, we can't help but respond with a wonder at his persistent vulnerability towards those he encounters even in the midst of increasing rejection and impending violence. How does Jesus keep from reacting out of fear and stress?

In the West we often overlook the way in which Jesus punctuates times of teaching, travelling and healing with 'Sabbath' times of rest and prayer. It isn't some spiritual *machismo* or 'otherworldly' martyr complex that permits him to embrace the suffering and hostility of humanity; it's his intimacy with God, his love-life of prayer that sustains and grounds him. As ministers to young people we too need time for communion with God. Our young people need us to take a moment to sit silently within the wide field of God's love in which we 'live and move and have our being' (Acts 17.28). Our young people need us to spend quiet moments receiving God's Spirit so that, like Jesus, our very bodies might be infused with hope, compassion and truthfulness.

Take a moment to set down this book and simply become aware of your surroundings. Allow your eyes to gently receive the light, colours and shapes around you without seeking to 'do' anything with what you see. Then gently close your eyes and turn your awareness to your ears. Allow yourself to receive the sounds and noises around you without judgement. Just let the sounds be what they are. Then take a moment to become aware of your body. Beginning with the top of your head, allow a gentle attention to move down your body to the soles of your feet. Allow yourself to notice places of tension or pain without passing judgement. Can you compassionately receive your physical self? Spend a few moments allowing your body to breathe and rest in the presence of God, just as it is.

Then when you are ready, take a moment to open your attention toward God. The God within whom we 'live and move and have our being'. Quietly turn your awareness to the presence of God within all that you see, all that you hear, and all that you feel. Don't force anything. Just for a few minutes allow yourself to open towards the presence of Divine Love within the reality of this moment – the way you might turn and receive the gaze of someone dear to you in the midst of a crowded room.

*   *   *

What was that experience like? Was it difficult to be in silence? Did your mind become full of different criticisms ('I'm not doing this right!', 'Nothing is happening!', 'I hate these kinds of exercises . . .')? Did you notice lots of commentary, day-dreaming and analysis? Was the time restful or did it make you agitated? It's difficult to stop our activity and simply be present to God. The inertia of our lives, the constant chatter of our minds make it challenging to simply sit in the present moment. This is true for everyone, even those who have spent most of their adult lives in silent prayer. And yet, do you notice that this time of seeking to be present to God is also, in some inexplicable way, nurturing?

The kind of prayer that invites us to dwell in the presence of God is called *contemplative prayer* or what some people call 'the prayer of the heart'. It's prayer in which we allow ourselves to become open and undefended before God, to dwell within God's Spirit without expectation. It's the disposition of Mary sitting at Jesus' feet attentive and listening. It's Jesus resting in the boat amidst the storm. It's the kind of prayer that the psalmist refers to when he writes, 'Be still and know that I am God.'

Although 'contemplative prayer' sounds like a lofty spiritual exercise reserved for saints, in reality it relies on a simple attitude of the heart that all of us have experienced. The word 'contemplative' means to 'be in the temple'. It means to rest in the temple or presence of God. When we seek to engage in contemplative prayer, all we are doing is seeking to rest attentively within the presence of God. Cistercian abbot and author Thomas Keating writes,

> We may think of prayer as thoughts or feelings expressed in words. But this is only one expression. Contemplative prayer is the opening of mind and heart – our whole being – to God, the Ultimate Mystery, beyond thoughts, words, and emotions. We open our awareness to God whom we know by faith is within us, closer than breathing, closer than thinking, closer than choosing – closer than consciousness itself.[4]

Just as our human relationships involve times of talking, listening and working together, any long-term relationship also involves moments of simply resting in the presence of one another. This is the same disposition we seek to incorporate in our relationship with God.

With three young, energetic kids, most of my time at home is spent helping with school work, organizing schedules, playing, preparing food, cleaning and doing the errands and odd jobs that keep a household running. My wife's time at home is even more of the same. Most days we both seek to incarnate a sense of gratitude and love as we go about the mundane tasks of domestic living, but as any parent knows, domestic life can quickly make us fatigued and cranky. Over the years a pattern has developed where, after the kids are asleep, Jill and I sit in the kitchen and spend an hour or two reflecting on the gifts and struggles of the day, purely enjoying the pleasure of each other's company. These moments with my wife expand my life. They are moments when I can let go of constricting stress and allow my perspective to enlarge beyond my own frustrations and concerns. Many evenings, after pouring out the events of the day or after sharing a particular experience of joy, frustration or deep pain, my wife and I will simply fall silent. The silence may last a minute or may last a half-hour. But in that silence, we merely rest in the intimate presence of one another and the mystery of our lives – neither of us feeling the need to speak or act. I have noticed, over the years, that these moments of silence are often the most intimate and healing moments of our marriage. They are moments when we rest in the reality of our relationship (be it painful or peaceful), the relationship that is being woven together beneath our words and actions.

Contemplative prayer is an invitation to enter into our deep relationship with God. It's an invitation to set aside our agendas and spiritual striving and simply allow ourselves to sit silently, vulnerable to God's presence within and around us. For the first 16 centuries of the Christian tradition, contemplative prayer referred to 'resting in God'.[5] We who seek to share the faith of Jesus within the energy of young people need this kind of spiritual rest if we're to be empowered to share the gospel.

Just like Jesus, our souls are drawn from time to time to deserted woodlands, quiet lakesides, cloistered spaces where we can let down our hearts to God. Deep within us is a desire to share the life of Jesus (not just the words of Jesus). We too seek time with the One Jesus trusted; the One who seeks to comfort our spirits, heal our barriers, arouse our generosity and remind us of our larger capacity to love. We are made to commune with God, to breathe and live God. Our hearts, bodies and souls yearn for space and time to sink down into God's love where we might discover an underground reservoir of mercy waiting within the striving activity of our lives. Those of us who seek to share the way of Jesus with young people need time sit unguarded before the Spirit of God.

Over the centuries, Christians have found many different ways to spend time dwelling in the presence of God. Some of these methods are unique to individuals, others have become practices that groups and communities have tended and written about for centuries. For the past 12 years I have practised and taught two basic, traditional forms of contemplative prayer to parents and people who minister with young people: *lectio divina* and centring prayer. After reading the description of each of these prayer methods, take ten minutes to actually engage in one of these prayers before you continue your reading. Give yourself permission to spend just ten minutes allowing God to minister to your spirit.

Lectio divina

Lectio divina is Latin for 'holy reading' and comes out of the Benedictine monastic tradition. This prayer can be described as experiencing God through Scripture. It's a classical form of prayer designed to gently draw a person into the depths of her or his own heart and there meet God. This form of prayer has for centuries been one of the principal methods by which Christians have been led into the experience of contemplation.

Lectio divina invites us into contemplative prayer by meditating on a particular biblical text. Before entering into the prayer it is first helpful to notice that there are many ways in which we read. We 'scan' the newspaper for information. We 'study' a book to increase our knowledge or hone our critical faculties. We become 'absorbed' in a good novel. When we engage in *lectio divina* we are not seeking to read the Bible for knowledge or seek instruction (although both of these may come), nor are we seeking the escape of a good story; instead we come to the words of the Bible seeking to be with God. We come to Scripture as if it were a meeting place, a secret rendezvous where we hope to spend some time with the One who loves us.

My wife and I dated in college before the days of e-mail. During the summers, when we were apart, we would write letters to one another. I still remember the excitement of running to the mailbox after each workday hoping to see a letter with my name written in Jill's handwriting. Each time I received a letter from my beloved, I would run down to my room, close the door and then slowly pore over her words. When I read a letter from Jill, it was very different from the way in which I engaged in other forms of reading. I wasn't seeking to catch up on the news as much as I was seeking to experience Jill. I was seeking to meet her in her letters, to receive her love, to feel her presence and be with her in some way.

When we engage in *lectio divina* we come to the words of the Bible as if they are words from a lover. We come to the text seeking to encounter God, seeking to make contact with God's love and God's presence. We come to Scripture trusting God's nearness, trusting God's desire to heal and transform us, expecting God to meet us just on the other side of Scripture.

At first the steps of this prayer might seem arbitrary and complicated. But as you engage in the prayer I think you will find the steps of *lectio divina* are quite natural (you may even notice that you have already practised a similar form of prayer or Bible reading on your own) and are designed to gently draw us into contemplative prayer. They are as follows:

- *Preparation.* Begin by finding a passage of Scripture to pray with. You can choose a passage based on a lectionary, a daily devotional, or by simply selecting a passage on your own. Make sure the Scripture is not too long. Next, find a quiet place in which to pray – some place where you won't be distracted or interrupted, a place where you feel safe and comfortable to open to God. Often it's helpful to light a candle or set out a sacred object, something beautiful that quiets your spirit and reminds you of God's nearness.
- *Silence.* Once you have found a place in which to pray, take a moment to simply rest, relaxing into God's presence. With each breath become aware of God's love for you. Say a simple prayer, offering yourself to God and welcoming whatever the Holy Spirit has for you in this time.
- *Reading.* Then begin prayerfully to read the text. Read the passage once to get oriented to the text, then read it slowly a second and third time, listening for a word or phrase that seems to shimmer or stand out in bold, a word that seems to address you. It may be a word that draws your attention through either attraction or repulsion.
- *Meditation.* Once a word or phrase has been given, gently repeat it within yourself, allowing the rest of the text to fall away. As you prayerfully repeat it, you may notice different thoughts, feelings and images that arise. Allow this word to touch all that arises – thoughts, hopes, memories, images and feelings. What do you notice? What is being offered?
- *Oration.* Let yourself express prayers of petition or gratitude as they arise. Your meditation on the word may uncover a place of pain or regret. Pray this to God. You may notice a person or situation that needs prayer. Go ahead and pray this to God. Honestly express your deepest thoughts, feelings and desires in dialogue with God. Pray yourself empty.

- *Contemplation.* Finally, allow yourself to simply rest in God. Like a child resting in her mother's lap, spent from crying. Lay down all of the insights, words and images that you've encountered and simply dwell in the presence of God. Sink down into God beneath all your thoughts and feelings.

As you engage in *lectio*, you may find that you have a different progression than the steps of prayer I have just laid out. For example, you may find yourself praying out all kinds of concerns at the beginning of the prayer. Or you may find yourself in an undefended place of rest and trust after reading the Scripture and only as you end the prayer do you have a word addressed to you from the text. All of this is appropriate. 'Pray as you can, not as you can't', Dom Chapman once said. You're merely seeking to come to the Scripture open and seeking to be with God. You read the words of Scripture. You rest for a period of time. You leave with a word addressed to you. The prayer is that simple.

Centring prayer

Although the term 'centring prayer' and its particular format only came into being within the last 40 years, the prayer is a summary of various silent prayer practices that can be traced back to the very beginnings of Christianity.[6] Again, you may find that you already have engaged in this form of prayer without realizing it. Centring prayer is a simplified form of contemplative prayer and draws on the latter steps of *lectio divina*. It's a form of prayer that trusts the direct and immediate availability of God, the 'indwelling Christ', nearer than our own heartbeat.

We live in a culture that increasingly lives in the 'head' – ideas, calculations, abstractions, theologies – and for many of us in ministry 'thinking' about God can often replace 'being' with God. For many of us, *lectio divina* can be a difficult form of contemplative prayer. In reading Scripture we immediately begin to analyse the text, looking for interesting bits of meaning, lesson plans or solutions to present-day problems. This kind of study and analysis of the Bible is a critical and necessary part of ministry and Christian living, but it can be a hindrance – even a form of resistance – as we seek to be open and present to God. Imagine a woman sitting on the front porch at the end of the day, calling to her husband inside the house saying, 'Work was so draining today. I couldn't wait to get home. Come sit next to me on the porch.' The husband then comes to the doorway and replies, 'Isn't it interesting how work takes up so much of our lives? I mean, here is this activity that we have to engage in to pay the bills, an activity that we hope will be satisfying at some level and yet at the end of the day we feel like we've been, as you say, "drained". Like something has been taken away from us or maybe that we've given a part of ourselves that we now notice is missing. Maybe that's why you say you couldn't wait to get home. It's like we leave our true selves at work and . . .' etc.

Imagine that for the next 30 minutes the husband stands in the doorway reflecting on his wife's words, the nature of work, all the while missing her invitation to come and sit and be with her. We may find in *lectio* that we do the same. We spend most of our prayer time fascinated by our thoughts and reflections on the words, so that we never really take time to come and sit and be with God.

In centring prayer we remove the temptation to spend our prayer time in thought and study (again, it's not that biblical study and reflection is wrong, just the opposite: it's necessary to the Christian life; it's just that in contemplative prayer we seek to set aside our study and reflection in order to be fully attentive to God's presence).

Centring prayer is a direct, immediate and deceptively simple form of silent prayer. The guidelines are as follows:[7]

- Sit comfortably in a space where you can open to God. Have a set time to pray – ten minutes or so is a good beginning. You may want to light a candle to help remind you of God's nearness.
- Before you begin the prayer, choose a sacred word as the symbol of your intention to be with God. This word expresses your desire to be in God's presence and yield to the movement of the Holy Spirit. The sacred word can be chosen during a brief period of prayer, asking the Holy Spirit to reveal a word

that is most suitable to you. Examples may include *Jesus, Lord, Abba, Love, Mercy, Stillness, Faith, Trust, Shalom, Amen*. Once you have selected a word, stick with it. Often people get caught up worrying whether their word feels right for them, wondering about the various meanings of their word, comparing their word to other words, or wondering if some other word might be more 'spiritual' and produce 'better' results. Don't take your word so seriously. Our word is simply a reminder of our desire to be with God. What's significant in this prayer is our intention (to be with God), not our particular word.

- It's now time to pray. Close your eyes and settle down for a moment. Allow rest and hospitality to come over your body. Welcome God into this time. Now briefly and silently introduce the sacred word as the symbol of your consent to God's presence and action within and around you. Thomas Keating suggests introducing the sacred word 'inwardly and as gently as laying a feather on a piece of cotton'.
- Almost immediately you will become aware of thoughts, memories, commentaries and images. When you notice your mind wandering, gently return to the sacred word. Thoughts are a normal part of centring prayer, yet by quietly returning to the sacred word, minimal effort is used to bring our attention back to God.
- At the end of the prayer period remain in silence with eyes closed for a minute or two. You may want to close with the 'Our Father' or some other formal prayer as a way of drawing the prayer to a close.

Centring prayer, like all forms of contemplative prayer, can often be frustrating. Most of us have difficulty being present to another person, much less God. We would prefer a God who is full of sights and sounds, a God who would capture our attention in prayer with words and insight. And yet God often communicates in 'sighs too deep for words' (Romans 8.26).

Often when I engage in centring prayer I become overly aware of my chattering mind. I have long moments when I forget I'm praying, my attention lost in a thousand thoughts. I find that I often don't 'get anything' out of the prayer period itself; however, over time I have noticed dramatic shifts in my sense of God, self and my commitment to following the way of Jesus. As a friend of mine once told me, in centring prayer, 'God is praying us'. We wait with listening hearts while God does the speaking in words that only the deep recesses of our heart can perceive.

Whatever the form, the purpose of contemplative prayer is not that we might experience blissful moments of peace or escape the anxious reality of our lives. We practise contemplative prayer so that we might become aware and receptive to the reality of life – even further, so that we might become more in touch with God's presence in the middle of life, of the Real within the real. We are seeking to make contact with God's love in the world, and coming into contact with love is not always peaceful. Like love itself, opening to the truth of God's presence can be painful, unearthing ignored questions and arousing nagging doubts. Moments of open, listening prayer not only help us to become aware of God, we also 'sober up' to the truth of ourselves. Seeking to dwell within the Spirit of God, we often touch into the truth of our own situation. We notice our exhaustion, our frustration, our sin, our neediness, or latent hope. Often the fruit of contemplative prayer is not in the prayer itself, rather it's in the softening of the heart that we experience in daily life. The Holy Spirit comforts and heals the deep wounds within us, emotional knots are revealed or loosened – we yield to God's transforming work in ways that are difficult for us to perceive. And yet there are other moments when we notice, almost tangibly, God's Spirit moving and breathing within us.

As I have practised contemplative prayer within youth ministry I have noticed that over time situations with teenagers that used to provoke great stress, feelings of inadequacy or frustration now seem just part of the ministry. I feel a greater ability to act out of love and honesty with kids who are disruptive or challenging. I trust more in God's presence, and I'm less likely to lean entirely on my own efforts or charisma.

TJ was a boy who I found difficult to work with. He had spent much of his teenage years being passed from one foster home to another. He was deeply wounded, needy for attention and yet possessed the energy of ten chimpanzees. Every time TJ showed up to a youth ministry meeting he would skateboard into the church building, crash into our classroom and then immediately begin talking at hyper-speed. Shifting back and forth in his seat he would shout out a steady barrage of wisecracks at a volume reserved for punk rock clubs. I found myself irritated and reactive around TJ and noticed I felt relieved when he didn't show up.

I wanted to find a different way to relate to TJ and soon moved my prayer time with the other youth ministry leaders to take place right before our meeting with the youth. Although TJ continued to be disruptive, over time I noticed that my times of contemplative prayer were creating greater space and patience within me to work with TJ. I perceived a growing sense of compassion for his situation and even noticed that his attention-getting tactics weren't much different from my own. I still had difficulty working with TJ and often had to set boundaries with him in order to facilitate the class, but as I spent each day surrendering myself and the ministry over to God I became more open to God's hope for TJ and less attentive to my own issues and frustrations.

Contemplative prayer does not take away the anxiety or problems within ministry. There are still plenty of times when I take on too much responsibility with kids, plenty of moments when I react out of anger or anxiety. Yet, these times of prayer have helped me to notice sooner when I have acted out of my own anxiety, pride or neediness rather than the truth and patience of God. Contemplative prayer has helped me mature in my faith and ministry and made me more aware of the true intention behind my words and actions with kids.

As ministers it's necessary that we spend regular periods of time in contemplative prayer. How can we share God if we don't spend time deepening our own relationship with God? Usually ten minutes in the morning is a good start. Just ten minutes! Sometimes, I find it helpful to begin my prayer time dedicating this time to the young people I serve. This gives me a reminder that this prayer is not only for my benefit, but is deeply connected to the people I serve.

Young people are not looking for adults who have better, more poetic or more reasoned beliefs. They are looking for adults who have experienced something, who trust something larger than themselves. They're looking for adults who 'have heard with their own ears, seen with their own eyes, and touched with their own hands' (1 John 1.1). Our young people need us to spend regular periods of time yielding to God's life and love. They need us to be grounded in a Source of life larger than our own fretful concern. They need adults whose lives are 'lit up', illumined by the awareness of God in the world. In this culture we often feel guilty for taking time to simply rest. It seems so inefficient, unproductive and useless. We tend to perceive ministry and the Christian life as a series of outward activities. We dismiss warnings from author and Episcopal priest Morton Kelsey that an efficiently busy life is 'more potentially destructive of spiritual growth than debauchery or alcohol or hard drugs'.

If we desire young people to trust the mystery of God revealed in Jesus Christ, then we need to inhabit the mysterious Being of God. We need to open to this spring of divine love from which our theologies, ethics and doctrines grow. For if our words and actions are not watered by the healing love of God, then our ministries will soon become dry and uninspired. Our hope, as I've previously stated, is not simply to teach kids a set of beliefs (belief is simply a stage on the way to knowing God). Our hope is that our young people might know God and trust the way of life that Jesus has emblazoned – a way of life in which one seeks to live in greater transparency to the reality of God and greater vulnerability to the presence of others. The theologies, ethics and doctrines we seek to share with young people are meaningless unless they are enchanted by this sacred life of God.

If we are to minister with young people, then like Jesus we must set aside regular moments to stop, let go of our hold on life, and let God love us. This is Jesus' desire for us. This is the intention of contemplative prayer. This is the way of life our young people long for us to live.

6

From prayer to presence

————⊷●⊶————

I continue to desire a more contemplative attitude towards youth ministry. I feel like it gives me licence to just be present to our young people without feeling guilty about programming. I am able to sit and truly listen to them and revel in what they share about their lives. I find I enjoy the end of the evening when the discussion is over and they hang out before being picked up by their parents. I get excited that they want to stay long enough to share what is going on in their life. I think contemplative practice has helped me see each of them as individuals and not as a collective group of 'teenagers'.

(Lawrence Molloy, youth pastor,
Our Lady Help of Christians Church, Newton,
Massachusetts)

Those who are unhappy have no need for anything in this world but people capable of giving them their attention. The capacity to give one's attention to a sufferer is a very rare and difficult thing; it is almost a miracle; it *is* a miracle.

(Simone Weil, *Waiting for God*)

The morning worship gathering was unremarkable. The sanctuary was about two-thirds full with approximately 200 people, most topped with grey hair. I made my way up the aisle and took a seat in the front pew. After perusing the pastel worship bulletin, I looked up and was surprised to find 15 or 20 teenagers sitting to my immediate left in a makeshift set of benches. I later found out that these were the youth 'bleachers' and were reserved as a special place for young people.

The service proceeded and after the sermon a small group of church elders came forward to serve Communion. The bread and wine were prayed over, the Spirit invoked, and a hymn sung. Congregants were then invited to come forward to share in the sacred elements. The always orderly Presbyterians had a system: starting with the back row, ushers directed people to rise and come to the communion table. As people filed forward I looked up and noticed one of the communion assistants standing directly in front of me. She was an elderly woman, somewhere in her late 70s, gussied up the way elderly Presbyterian women often are with a silk jacket, white blouse, flowered skirt and matching heels. She stood waiting patiently, carefully steadying a heavy platter of bread. As people advanced, she greeted them with a smile and in a quavering voice said, 'This is the Body of Christ, given for you.' There was a kindness and gentleness in her greeting and I soon found myself gazing at her throughout the ritual.

Finally it was my turn to come forward. After taking the elements I sat back down and returned my eyes to the elderly woman. I was startled by what I saw. Instead of the serene and gentle smile that had greeted me just a moment earlier, the woman's face was pained and shuddering with emotion. Her head bowed, jaw knotted, she gripped the communion plate, struggling to keep her composure. I moved to the edge of the pew and prepared to step in when all of a sudden up to the front of the sanctuary came the gangly group of teenagers. They rambled up in a whispering, giggling, nudging mob, causing the usher to spew numerous 'shushes' while quickly sorting them into an orderly line. The young man placed at the front stepped forward and waited to receive the bread. I sat pensive, uncertain if I should offer help, when suddenly the woman looked up, her eyes pouring tears, held the bread before the young man and said, 'The Body of Christ, given for you, Thomas.' The next young person approached and again in a voice tender with weeping she said, 'The Body of Christ, given for you, Sarah.' As each youth approached she made the effort to look at them through her tears and slowly offer them the bread, speaking their names with love.

At the end of the service the associate pastor accompanied me to a meeting of the 15 adults who served in the youth ministry.

I had asked to interview this group in order to learn about their efforts to incorporate contemplation in youth ministry. I sat down and looked across the circle of chairs and quickly noticed the same elderly woman who had served Communion. I introduced myself, and found her name was Mildred. The meeting had yet to start, so I leaned forward and curiously prodded, 'Mildred, you seemed to have a lot of emotion during Communion this morning . . .'

'Yes,' she replied, smiling self-consciously. 'It took me by surprise.'

'I could see that you have a lot of care for the young people.' I prodded some more.

'Well, actually, most of those kids I've never met before.' I gave her a quizzical look.

'You see, I was asked to serve in the youth ministry by praying for the kids. I'm too old to run around with them, but I told Jen [the associate pastor] I could pray for them. Well, Jen took Polaroid photos of all the kids and asked them to write their names on the back along with a prayer concern. All of us adults trade these cards each week so that each of us gets time to pray for each kid. That was three years ago. Every morning, for three years, I take out my photos and spend time just looking at the faces of those kids. Then I read their concerns and pray for them.

'This morning was the first time I've ever been asked to assist in Communion. I felt so honoured. And then suddenly I see these young faces coming toward me . . .' She welled up with tears and bowed her head for a few moments.

'I have beheld those faces for three years praying for them and their futures. And then suddenly here they are in front of me and I'm handing the bread of Christ to them. It was just too much, too overwhelming. I tried to stop each of them and just look at them and hug them with my eyes. I just felt so honoured.'

There is no greater gift we can give our young people than our full and loving attention. I often picture the face of the woman from Westminster Presbyterian when I remember the way in which I seek to be present to young people in my own life. Notice that she felt 'honoured' to be with the youth – in the same way that she felt 'honoured' to hold the bread of Christ. She was open and fully present, greeting each young person with a sense of gratitude and compassion. She was patient and slow, taking time to 'behold' each young person. Her ability to receive these kids with love and compassion was directly connected to her times of prayer.

Over the past ten years I've worked with numerous youth ministry programmes and have become convinced that the more we engage in contemplative prayer the more we are able to be present to young people. In spending time 'beholding God' we learn to 'behold' young people (and others). This transformation from anxiety to love takes place, I believe, as we learn to just 'be' with God. Soon the attitude and presence we seek to embody in our relationship with God begins to permeate our relationships with young people. We develop a growing awareness of the presence of God within young people and soon notice that the patience we bring to contemplative prayer is also available in our relationships with youth. *It's this movement from prayer to presence, from being open and available to God to being transparent and accessible before teens, that is the real work of ministry.*

It's easy to imagine a very different experience during my visit to Westminster Presbyterian. You might expect that in most churches people could become flustered and irritated by a gangly group of teenagers swarming down upon the communion table. In fact, five years earlier at this same church youth and children were dismissed from the worship service before it ever began. When the pastor demanded that the youth stay for at least the first half of the service, a large number of congregants became irate. It was only when the senior pastor threatened to quit that the elders of the church allowed youth and children to remain in the service. The transformation that I witnessed within Mildred and other church members was dramatic. When I asked the staff and adult volunteers to account for the shift in how youth were perceived and treated within the congregation they pointed to their times of individual and small group contemplative prayer dedicated to youth.

The conversion at Westminster did not go unnoticed by the young people. Not only were more youth attending the church; more young people were participating in worship, teaching in the Sunday school programme and serving in leadership positions.

More importantly, the youth felt welcomed into a community of faith that was very different from the way they experienced life at school and in their neighbourhoods. I remember meeting a 15-year-old boy named Nate who often came to worship on his own. When I asked him 'Why?' he told me:

> When I leave my house to go to church I usually begin walking like I walk to school. But then as I come around my block and see the church building I start smiling. And by the time I reach the kerb in front of the church I'm giggling and then when I reach the front door of the church I'm just about ready to fall down laughing, because I know as soon as I open that door all of these older folks are going to look over and see me and start smiling. Then they're going to come over and hug me and they're going to ask me all kinds of questions and they're going to want me to sit by them in the service. And that just cracks me up.

It was no surprise when I ran into Nate five years later and found out he was working for a Christian organization that serves the rural poor. How could he resist participating within a community and a way of life that made him feel so valued?

If you look back over your own life you may find that the moments where you were most deeply impacted were moments when you were in the presence of someone who was fully present to you. Give yourself the space right now to reflect on the last time you felt someone completely present and available to you. When was the last time you felt fully received by another person with compassion and care? What was it like?

*   *   *

Sadly, for many of us there are precious few moments among our many human interactions when we feel someone is fully present to us – even within our marriages and families. Most of us have so few experiences when we have felt truly seen or listened to. And yet, when these interactions do happen, they can be transformative. I'm convinced that many of us are Christians today because some person or group of people listened to us, saw us, received and delighted in us. This is the kind of presence our youth long for, this is the kind of presence Jesus embodied, this is the kind of presence we seek to incarnate in order to love young people into faith.

How do we offer this kind of presence to young people? How do we move from contemplative prayer to contemplative presence within our ministries with youth? The first step might be noticing that contemplative awareness is something we're all familiar with – all of us have experienced moments of contemplation. All of us have had moments, like Mildred, of being fully present to another person. It's that full-hearted presence that comes over a parent as they gaze upon their newborn baby. It's the quiet appreciation that descends on old friends as they sit together without speaking. It's neighbours sitting on their front porch, taking in the sights and sounds of the closing day. It's the elders from the temple sitting around 12-year-old Jesus listening in wonder and amazement.

Contemplation is an attitude of the heart, an all-embracing hospitality to what is. Contemplation is a natural human disposition – it's the way in which we approached the world as children: vulnerable, open, awake to the present moment. We all have experience of being contemplatively present. Even as our adult minds become distracted and burdened with worry we still receive times of contemplation, times of simple presence. These are unrehearsed moments when a deep sense of gratitude falls upon us and we find ourselves without need or want, satisfied and reverent at the Mystery of life. Like love, contemplative awareness is not something we achieve; rather it comes as a gift, simply to be received. And yet there are ways in which we can be more open and available to contemplation within our relationships with youth.

7

Being with young people

To listen tenderly and lovingly to the petty foibles, the painful longings, the relentless thirst for God that crowd into the consciousness of each of us is to listen, in fact, to God's own longing to live among and transform us. To listen to one another in this way is indeed to be a lover of souls.

(Wendy Wright, 'Desert Listening',
Weavings, May/June 1994)

A contemplative approach to youth ministry has helped me see young people in a totally different way. I have 'new eyes'. I notice that as I give myself to stillness and contemplation, I see all things differently. I am able to hold them and 'breathe them in'. I believe I communicate to the kids by the way I am present to them – kids have told me that in times of need, it isn't what I say to them as much as the way in which I'm present to them. Previously, I was always thinking about what I was going to say to them; now I am able to simply be with them, listen and then respond in faith.

(Tammy Clark, youth pastor, Valparaiso First
United Methodist Church, Valparaiso, Indiana)

As Christians we seek to make ourselves more and more available to contemplation. We want to move from prayer to presence; from receiving God in prayer, to receiving God within our relationships with others. What does it mean to be present to the young people we serve? What would it look like to develop contemplative presence within our ministries? My friend, Frank

Rogers at Claremont School of Theology, has laid out a description of being human that may best describe contemplative presence.[8] He expresses it as 'seeing and being seen, hearing and being heard, being moved by others and allowing others to be moved by us, responding with acts of kindness and receiving acts of kindness', and finally 'embodying a sense of delight in all our interactions'. I want to utilize Rogers' categories of seeing, hearing, being moved to compassion, acting in kindness and delighting to help us get a sense of what it means to relate to youth from a place of love.

Seeing

Franciscan priest, Richard Rohr, writes that transformation in the spiritual life 'is about seeing'.[9] It's about learning to see with the eyes of Jesus. As we bring contemplative awareness to our relationships with young people, the first thing we seek to do is simply see them. We love young people by seeing them as they are, not as the culture judges them to be or as we hope them to be. It's difficult for us to look at a young person (or any person for that matter) without judgement. It's difficult simply to receive a young person just as they present themselves without verbalizing or internalizing some sort of commentary. Most often when we see a group of youth we immediately begin to assess them: 'That freshman boy needs counselling, that one dresses too provocatively, that girl must have rich parents . . .'

Seeing is our first language. For most of us, it's the first way in which we make contact with the world. My daughter, Grace, is 16 months old. If you were here with me and she came into the room she would look at you a long time. Her eyes would be clear, open and vulnerable. She would examine your facial expression, take note of your body posture, and closely watch your reactions to her. When Grace sees someone, she sees them. She receives them through her eyes. All of us know this way of seeing, all of us have looked with Grace's eyes. It's these same open eyes that we seek to inhabit when we encounter youth.

It's clear to me through the New Testament that people felt seen by Jesus. And that for Jesus, it was his willingness to openly see people (particularly those who often went unseen and unnoticed) that was at the heart of his ministry. When Jesus enters the town of Nain he is accompanied by his disciples and a large crowd. You can imagine the activity, conversation and sense of excitement that surrounded him as he came to the town's entrance. As the teacher and his followers enter Nain, they encounter a funeral procession. A young man has died and his body is being carried outside of the city gates closely followed by his grieving, widowed mother and a large crowd of mourners. Luke writes, 'When the Lord saw her, he had compassion for her . . .' (Luke 7.13).

Jesus sees the woman. He takes the woman in through his eyes. He sees and receives her grief. Out of this seeing arises compassion and later a healing act. But it is the seeing that comes first. Later in Luke's Gospel, Jesus tells the story of the prodigal son, and the same movements will be repeated. The younger son walks up the road to his father's house confused, hungry and downcast. The passage reads, 'But while he was still far off, his father saw him and was filled with compassion; he ran, put his arms around him and kissed him.' The father sees his son, notices his son's figure and dejected posture. Compassion arises and he responds with an act of reconciliation.

When we seek to be contemplatively present to young people we seek to see them through the eyes of love. We look at them the way you might look at your child or beloved as they sleep. It's such a sweet pleasure to gaze upon someone as they sleep. It's a time of beholding them, of setting aside words and roles and allowing your eyes to rest upon them, taking in and enjoying who they are. I remember travelling with a particularly difficult group of teens to do a summer service project. We stopped to sleep in a church for the night and after unloading the vans the kids went berserk. They were racing down the aisles of the sanctuary with wheelchairs, putting on choir robes, hiding within the pipe organ, and climbing over the pews. Immediately I became angry. I went beyond disciplining them and soon was shouting at them with biting remarks. I got them into their sleeping bags, turned out the lights and demanded they go immediately to sleep.

One hour later I was still agitated and irritable and couldn't sleep. I felt badly about how I had treated the youth. I got out of my bedding and walked around the sanctuary. Kids were sleeping in pews, in the aisle and up by the altar. I walked slowly and knelt down beside each young person, gazing on them as they slept. I noticed their innocence. I remembered the pain that many of these kids carried – several of them were foster kids, abandoned by their parents. I suddenly felt compassion for them. They were excited to be on a trip, to get away from their families, to travel with their friends. I had been so aware of my own fatigue, of my concern with 'messing' up the church building, that I hadn't seen how the kids were excited to move their bodies. They were eager to play and run and release the pent-up energy from a day of sitting on a bus. I could have been more aware of their need to move and more straightforward in asking them to respect the church property.

That night I sat next to each sleeping face and simply looked at each young person, seeking to see them through Jesus' eyes. The next morning when we gathered to begin the day with prayer, I apologized for my outburst. I allowed the youth to see my own frustration and struggle as a youth leader. I told them that although I needed to remind them to care for the church building, I didn't need to yell at them with such meanness. I was surprised to see lots of forgiving smiles around the group. Then one youth responded, 'I've never heard an adult apologize before.' Then another spoke up, 'I guess we owe you an apology as well. You were tired from driving all day and probably were worried about being responsible for the building. Sorry we weren't more careful.'

When was the last time you looked at young people openly, without judgement or expectation? When was the last time you tried to look at someone with the eyes of God? When was the last time a young person felt seen by you? When have you allowed young people to really see you as you are? Can we look at young people with soft eyes? Can a young person come into our churches or ministries and be seen? Who might our young people become if every Christian they encounter 'beholds' them with eyes of love?

Hearing

To be contemplatively present to young people also means to listen. It means opening our ears to the words and feelings that young people speak. In the church we like talking, in fact it may be our primary practice. We forget that the majority of Jesus' teaching came after listening to the request or question of another person. As ministers we feel it's our job to talk. Often our whole youth programme, our activities, music, snacks and outings are all designed to help kids sit and listen to us talk. We rarely turn it around and seek to create programmes designed to help us listen to young people. And yet, I bet if you looked over your life, you could recall very few words from the countless sermons, lectures, speeches and conversations you have heard. In contrast, I would wager you remember most of the moments when you felt deeply heard and listened to by another person. It's almost a conversion experience in this day and age to be authentically heard by another person. So many of us don't really listen to others; what we really do is nod our heads, waiting for our turn to speak. Or when we do listen, we listen with an agenda, a filter. We listen for 'the right answer', we listen to see if they can repeat back what we've told them. We ignore or become uninterested in the words of young people when they don't fit our lesson plan. And yet, what would it be like for us to listen to young people openly, without preparing our response? What would it be like for young people to be truly heard within our churches and com-munities of faith? What if we trusted St Francis, who told his followers to 'preach the gospel, and if necessary, use words'?

I once led an exercise with a group of teenagers in which I asked them to remember a time when they felt deeply heard. I then asked them to share a word that captured how it felt. I wrote down their words:

Relief
Affirmed
Held
Cared for
Loved

Relevant
Freed up
Overwhelmed
Eternal
Expanded
Humbled
Important
Like God was present

Imagine if you were heard, deeply listened to, within every relationship. Who would you become? Take a moment to remember
an experience when you felt heard, a moment in which someone
listened to you openly, without an agenda? What was that like?

*   *   *

Recently a group of teenagers from a rough, poverty-stricken area
of San Francisco were asked to write essays about peace. The
project was funded as a response to the terrorist attack on the
World Trade Center. Instead of writing about peace, the youth
ended up writing about violence – it turned out this was much
closer to their experience. When the essays were finished the publisher asked the youth to come up with a title for the book. They
decided to call it *Waiting to be Heard.* This phrase comes to me
often when I encounter young people: waiting to be heard. If we
seek to share the presence of Christ with young people, we need
to let go of all our words, admonitions and advice, and simply
be with young people and listen to them. Listen to them in the
same way that we yearn to be listened to. Listen to them with
the patient ears of Jesus. Dietrich Bonhoeffer summarizes the
importance of ministry through listening:

> The first service that one owes to others in the fellowship
> consists in listening to them. Just as love to God begins with
> listening to His Word, so the beginning of love for our
> brothers and sisters is learning to listen to them. Christians,
> especially ministers, so often think they must always con-
> tribute something when they are in the company of others.

They forget that listening can be a greater service than speaking. Many people are looking for an ear that will listen. They do not find it among Christians, because these Christians are talking where they should be listening. But the person who can no longer listen to others will soon be no longer listening to God either. This is the beginning of the death of the spiritual life, and in the end there is nothing left but spiritual chatter and clerical condescension arrayed in pious works. Christians have forgotten that the ministry of listening has been committed to them by the One who is the great listener and whose work they should share. We should listen with the ears of God that we may speak the Word of God.[10]

Moved to compassion

When we take the time to see and hear young people, most often we find compassion rising within us. When we see with the eyes of Jesus and hear with the ears of Jesus, we soon find ourselves feeling with the heart of Jesus. One of the tasks of the adolescent period is to recruit people who care for them. Young people are moving outside their family circles, looking for friends, mentors and communities who care for them. What's tragic today is that so few young people are able to attract adults and communities who have the interest or time to spend with them.

When we seek to be present to young people, we not only see and hear them, we also seek to let down the walls of our heart and allow ourselves to be moved by them. As ministers with youth, we seek to have soft hearts, hearts that can be touched by the joy, confusion, loneliness, anger or tears of young people.

It's hard for those of us who minister with young people to feel the struggle of being young. It's easy for us to trivialize their pain and experience. Yet, we ourselves know that our lives are still marked by many of the pains and joys of our own adolescence. Can we allow ourselves to be moved by the young people in our lives? Can we stop and take the time to simply feel life from their perspective?

The most profound witness of the power of open-hearted presence occurred while I was leading a high school youth group. I was conducting a discussion on the difficulty of talking about our faith with people outside of Christianity. To help stimulate the discussion I set up, with suggestions from the young people, a role-play. The scene was simple: a high school cafeteria. One person, hostile to Christianity, was having lunch next to another young person who was reading a Christian devotional. I placed a table up front with two chairs and then asked for volunteers to play the two roles and allow the conversation to be a sort of spontaneous drama. Immediately Daniel stood up and took the seat of the person hostile to the faith. Then Sarah stood and took the seat of the Christian, reading a devotional. We started the drama and soon Daniel was ridiculing Sarah for her faith, claiming Christianity was a psychological crutch. Sarah, playing the role of the devout Christian, did her best to convince Daniel's character that the faith was more than just psychological comfort, but Daniel was persistent. Soon Sarah became flustered, and in line with the rules of the role-play, raised her hand and asked for someone to take her place.

Julie, a freshman, stepped up and began defending the Christian faith using different Bible verses to back her claims. Daniel, however, was ruthless, 'The Bible was made up just like all myths are made up. How can you believe in a God you've never seen? How can you claim this God is good when there is so much suffering in the world?' His emotion became so vivid that it became clear to me and the group that Daniel was no longer playing a role-play. His anger and questions were his own. I became worried that the exercise was getting out of hand, but I didn't know how to close it gracefully.

Julie raised her hand and this time Sam came up and tried to respond to Daniel's questions. Daniel became even more upset, and setting aside all pretences of the role-play, he unloaded, 'Listen, I was born in South Central, California – one of the roughest parts of LA. When I was four years old my best friend and I were walking to the park when a gun-fight broke out. We stood frozen just watching these gang kids shooting at each other. My friend Benjamin got hit in the chest by a stray bullet. I sat there screaming and crying and watched him die. Now you tell me God is good and loving? What kind of God allows a four-year-old kid to die like that?'

The room became starkly quiet. None of us knew how to respond. Sam quietly raised his hand. For a moment everyone stayed still, then Jake stood up and said, 'I'll take Sam's place.' Jake was the last guy I wanted to respond to Daniel's outburst. Five months earlier Jake had been arrested for burgling houses for drug money. His sentence was to attend an outdoor rehabilitation programme deep in the mountains of Idaho where, after living with other youth offenders in plastic tarp tents, he was sent out alone to spend a week in the wilderness to survive by his own wits. Jake was a big, strong kid who had attended church to get away from his parents and had shown little interest in the Christian faith. I was worried that he would take this opportunity to join Daniel in creating a scene and ridiculing Christianity. But for some reason, I didn't stop him from heading to the front of the room.

After walking up to the makeshift stage Jake removed the table, turned his chair and sat facing Daniel with open, steady eyes. There was a minute or so of silence as Jake continued to sit, relaxed and patient, just gazing at Daniel. Many of us felt awkward and I stood there, unsure whether I should interrupt. Then Daniel jumped in, and as if the role-play was continuing, began to accost Jake, 'So what do you have to say? That my friend Benjamin went to a better place? That this was part of God's plan? That God makes us suffer so that we'll turn to him? How can you possibly believe all this crap about God being a God of love?'

Jake just sat there. I assumed Jake was planning a response, when gradually Daniel quieted, sat still and returned Jake's gaze. And then something broke. Daniel's hard expression softened, his eyes searched Jake's and then I noticed what he was looking at. There were tears on Jake's face. Quietly, without looking away from Daniel, Jake let tears fall down his face. Daniel gazed at Jake in wonder for a moment, then his eyes swelled with tears and he lowered his head. Slowly, Jake stood up, raised Daniel from his chair and hugged him. After a few minutes they both stepped down and returned to the group. Jake never spoke a word.

The whole group sat stunned, unsure about what they had just seen. I encouraged the group to sit in silence for a moment, offered a short prayer and dismissed the class. Two weeks later,

Daniel began showing up to church – not just for youth activities but for morning worship. He came to Bible studies and served on the leadership team for the youth ministry. I never asked him about that night when Jake felt his tears, but I'm convinced that Jake was the presence of Christ to Daniel. His willingness to see, hear and feel Daniel's pain was the Good News that Daniel longed to encounter.

When was the last time you were moved by a young person's situation? When was the last time you felt joy or pain in empathy with a young person? Youth ministers strive to be people who are easily moved by the experience of adolescents, we're moved by their joy as well as their suffering. We have hearts that savour the energy, questions, struggles and sufferings of young people. Like Jesus, we find that through seeing, hearing and being with kids, we cultivate an open-hearted compassion for the struggles of young people. With every young person we encounter we find compassion rising up within us the way it did for the father when he noticed his lost son walking up the road, the way it did for the Samaritan when he looked upon the traveller beaten and hurting at the side of the road, the way it did for Jesus who saw the eager faces of the children, turned to the disciples and said, 'Let them come to me, do not stop them . . .'

Act with kindness

When we allow ourselves to be moved by the experience of young people, it's only natural to respond with acts of kindness. Just as the good Samaritan sees the man in the ditch, feels compassion and works to help the poor traveller, so we too are invited to engage in simple, ordinary actions that foster healing and encouragement.

Acts of kindness are moments in which we embody the love of God. Our kindness toward young people is a way of blessing them, a way of caring for them and letting them know they are valued. Kindness often takes place in small, hidden acts. We see these small acts of kindness in Jesus: making wine for a wedding party, giving bread and fish to a hungry crowd, cleaning the feet of the disciples, preparing breakfast on the beach for his friends.

The love of God is often more powerful and transformative in these small acts of love than in the lights, energy and charisma of large youth outreach events. What if we became more aware of the small ways in which we engage young people? What if our ministry was about giving rides home, sharing snacks, opening doors, helping carry book bags, and giving compliments when a young person has taken great care in their appearance? These small acts of kindness are little blessings, balms that heal the many mean and belittling messages that young people receive throughout each day.

As Christians we have always known that we're to act with kindness towards others, but when our deeds of charity come from a greater sense of God's presence we are able to bring our whole selves to the task. We are able to engage in these acts of love with a greater sense of Jesus' companionship. Suddenly they become not just moments of service but moments when we are being expanded and nurtured by God. We become aware, as Jesus suggests, that in these acts of love we're not just carrying book bags for a young person, we're also making contact with Jesus: 'When you do it for the least of these . . . you did it to me' (Matthew 25.40). We begin to feel more and more that we're participating in God's mission of love, rather than serving some moral ideal.

At one church where I served as the volunteer youth minister, church members would provide a Sunday dinner for the youth. There was always salad, a main course, dessert and drinks. Each Sunday the other youth ministry volunteers and I would carefully set up the tables, lay out the silverware and arrange the food in preparation for the arrival of the youth group. As the kids arrived we were intentional about greeting each youth by name, often giving them a hug and then inviting them to sit at the table. Meals would often last up to an hour and were filled with conversation and laughter. Many kids told us that it was the only 'real food' (as opposed to fast food, or microwave dinners) they received all week.

After dinner we'd play games, sing, pray and engage in Bible study . . . but as I look back on my time at that church I'm convinced that it was the care we put into greeting kids and serving them dinner that probably was the most effective communication of the Christian life. These dinners were filled with small acts of kindness and care directed toward the young people each week. If I interviewed the kids who came through that ministry over the five years I served there, I bet they wouldn't remember many of the lessons we taught, but I'm sure they would remember our times of eating, talking and laughing together around a table prepared with love and care.

When we take the time to be present and open to youth, we find that our actions are less frenetic, less about meeting some outside expectation, and less about us. Instead, the emphasis is on doing what's needed, and responding in love to the real situation before us. One of the 'icons' I keep before me as a reminder of how I seek to minister with young people occurred a couple of years ago while Christmas shopping.[11] Despite my intention to keep the celebration of Jesus' birth restful and relational, I found myself three days before Christmas rushing through a mall frantically searching for something for my wife. Having successfully located the perfect gift, I sat in the 'food court' of the mall wolfing down Chinese food. Suddenly into the cluster of brightly lit food stalls came ten developmentally disabled folks accompanied by two assistants with sweatshirts that read, 'The Redwoods Group Home'. In contrast to the hustling and harried shoppers these folks lumbered, otherworldly, through the tables and crowds, smiling and sometimes clapping hands or yelling with genuine pleasure at the sights and smells of the eating arena.

With slow and careful effort the assistants helped each person decide on the food they wanted to purchase, stand in line, order a meal, pay for the meal and then carry the food back to a table. The assistants were patient and spent much of the time conversing and sharing in the excitement of the disabled folks who were ecstatic about the personal sovereignty they were afforded amidst so many tasty delights. The assistants patiently helped people get their food and get seated before serving themselves. There was one man with Down's syndrome, however, who shook off every offer of help by the assistants. He knew what he wanted and he wanted to do it by himself. The assistants acquiesced, and watching from a safe distance let him walk to the McDonald's booth and stand in line. The young man stood with import and dignity holding some sort of worn red and yellow coupon in his hand. When he reached the front of the line he handed the paper over to the cashier, spoke loudly, and gestured toward a stack of various cups and the coffee machine. The cashier obliged and a few moments later the young man returned to his friends holding a giant 32-ounce cup of coffee, his face beaming with pride.

I stood up to hit one last store before going home. After my final purchase I headed for the parking lot through two smoky glass doors and quickly found myself behind the 12 folks from the group home. Rain was coming down in buckets and the assistants had their charges staying dry under the eaves of the mall entrance. One by one the assistants accompanied their group across the slippery sidewalk into a waiting van. Back and forth the assistants went, their clothes weighed down with water as they sought to keep their charges dry. As I stepped around the group I noticed the young man with the McDonald's coffee. He was bent over his hard-won brew, sheltering it from the downpour. Then, without any apparent direction from the assistants, he took off from underneath the side of the building, bolting for the warmth and security of the van. It was a spontaneous act, and halfway across the sidewalk he stopped, startled by the heavy rain, turned and decided to return to the cover of the mall eaves. One of the assistants saw him turn back and yelled to him to continue his route toward the vehicle. Increasingly shocked and confused by the soaking water he twisted his body toward the voice of the assistant with a quick jerk that caused the 32-ounce coffee cup to slip from his hands and break open against the wet concrete. Across the grey pavement the caffeine steamed and flowed like a mud slide. The young man froze, took in the sight of his lost purchase and began to cry. Soon his body gave way and he slumped down into the brown puddle. It was a pitiful sight – this young man wailing mournfully, sitting in a growing pond of coffee, the dark rain soaking his clothes.

We all looked on in helpless sympathy when one of the assistants, a twenty-something woman, stepped out from the van. She ran over to the young man, sat down in the cold wet coffee, wrapped her arm around him, placed his head on her shoulder and let him cry. For several minutes she sat there with the patience of God, just holding the young man while rain poured down. I stood transfixed, somehow aware that I was gazing upon one of the deep spiritual truths of our relationship to one another, of our capacity to care for one another, of the way in which we participate in the power of God's healing love through gentle acts of solidarity and kindness. When the man had calmed, the young assistant took his hand, lifted him up from the concrete and lead him to the front passenger seat of the van. She helped him with his seat belt, gave him a kiss and shut the door. Her clothes slung with water, her jeans stained brown, she stepped into the van, slid the door shut, then squeezed her body into the back seat.

The assistant from the Redwoods Group Home wasn't seeking to follow some prescribed method of behaviour. She wasn't following a programme or curriculum in her actions towards the young man. Her actions were natural, flowing from her willingness to be present to the people she served. She chose to sit in the teeming rain because she saw the young man, heard his cry, and felt her heart go out to him. All of the assistants had responded to the needs of the disabled people with a series of small acts of kindness – from helping people get their food, to finding chairs and tables, to walking folks through the rain and finally to giving a troubled person the best seat in the van. This is the same way in which we seek to respond to young people – with actions that flow from relationship, from attentiveness, from compassion and transparency to God's love.

Contemplation isn't just being still. As Parker Palmer once wrote, 'At root, contemplation and action are the same.'[12] As our youth ministry becomes infused with contemplative prayer and awareness, the effect is not more prayer and silence; instead what begins to emerge is authentic action. Activities within the youth ministry no longer are chosen frantically from resource books, they no longer are prescribed from the outside. Instead, as we widen our awareness, our actions with youth become more guided by their needs and the movement of the Holy Spirit. Being prayerfully present to kids enlarges our capacity to act out of love rather than anxiety. Contemplative awareness nurtures our creativity and draws us to act from the heart. We find ourselves *responding* more and *reacting* less.

Think about the last time you received an act of kindness. What was this experience like? How often do young people experience kindness within your community of faith? What would your relationship and ministry with young people be like if you attended to the small actions that reveal the kindness of Jesus?

Delight

Jesus spent most of his life in wonder. He stood in wonder at the beauty of the natural world, the pain and suffering of people, and the faith of strangers. He stood in wonder at the little ones, the marginalized and discarded children. He stood amazed at the willingness of people to repent and participate in God's work in the world. He stood enchanted by God's love and devotion to humanity.

One of the signs that indicate we're called to serve young people is that we are amazed by them. It may be that our best qualification as youth ministers is that we are easily delighted by the presence of young people. As ministers, we not only take the time to see, hear and be moved by their experience, we also infuse every interaction with a sense of delight. People who hope to share the Christian faith with teenagers are people who delight in young people. Within each interaction we seek to get a glimpse of their beauty, their gifts and their belovedness in God.

There may be nothing more pleasurable, more nurturing and even healing than being in the presence of someone who genuinely delights in you. I see this in my children. They want me to watch them do a back-flip off the couch, to look at a drawing of a boat, to eat the cookie they've just made – they call my attention to themselves over and over each and every day. What they seek are not pointers on gymnastic form, or comparisons with other visual artists, or comments on the texture of the cookie they've just made. What they want is for me to yell, 'Wow! What a flip!' They want me to look at their drawings and say, 'I love the way you drew that mast and look here at the anchor, why that looks so real.' They long for me to taste their new cookie creation, close my eyes and say, 'This is incredible! I could eat 20 of these!' What my kids want, what we all want, is delight. They want, just as we all want, to feel that their presence, their gifts, their expressions, their yearnings, are a source of joy in the world.

This is the spirit of contemplative presence. When I truly seek to be prayerfully open and available to a young person I seek to see them. To hear them. To be moved by their experience. To respond with kindness. And then, in all my interactions I seek to embody a sense of delight in their presence in the world – even in the midst of suffering or great brokenness. This is what it means to love like Jesus. This is the good news that Jesus calls us to share.

*   *   *

Love, as Jean Vanier once wrote, 'is to reveal the beauty of another person to themselves'.[13] This is why we seek to be fully present to young people. Because when a young person is seen they feel valued. When they are heard, they feel respected. When someone is moved by their situation, they feel loved. When they receive kindness, they feel cared for. And when others delight in their existence, they sense the very breath of God.

Youth ministry is about holding a young person's deepest identity until they are able to see it for themselves. We hold on to the knowledge that they are the beloved of God, that they have gifts that enrich the world, and that their presence is itself a cause for celebration. We hold this understanding of young people until they can hold it for themselves. We seek to reveal their beauty back to them until they see it, until they believe it, until they can live from it grounded in God's love.

What would it mean if the goal of our ministries was simply to be prayerfully present to young people – allowing them to be fully themselves? Could we trust that our presence is enough? How would we treat youth if we weren't trying to convince them of the importance of the faith, the worthiness of Jesus, the necessity of the Church? What would happen if we sought to minister to young people through our ears, through our presence, through silent prayer and an open heart? What would that kind of radical acceptance evoke in young people? Contemplative youth ministry is about deepening our presence to both God and young people. Although contemplative ministry is grounded in prayer and openness to God, the fruit of this time is in our increasing ability to be present, open and available in all our relationships.

Taking time to engage in contemplative prayer prepares us for wonder and amazement. When we stop and slow down we are open and available to see the miracle of living life and the power of God's presence in the world. Like Jesus, we let go of any attempts to manipulate or pressure young people into the faith, and instead find ourselves increasingly trusting the slow work of God.

8

Remembering

———◆◆◆———

My dedication to the youth in my midst has deepened, and they have become not a responsibility but a gift and a treasure in my life in a new way. When I listen to them, I *listen* to them. Because I am listening more, I care more, and because I care more, they talk more. Contemplative practice has changed my paradigm about God and so I am a better model for the youth I encounter. I have learned that God is also within me, that I am beloved, that I can do all things with God, and that Love always wins, always. How can that not impact the youth I'm with? I am able to be present for JT who has been in foster homes while his mother was recovering from alcohol abuse. JT knows he is beloved and that I care. I am able to be present to JT because I am centred with God. When I am with him, I am not thinking about ten other things I could/should/ought to be doing next.

> (Laurie Rodney, educational consultant, parent and
> youth ministry volunteer, Church of the Redeemer,
> Cleveland, Ohio)

The lightest and most ordinary encounter with the laughing God happens in the little instant of remembering love after we have been forgetful. For me it is one of the most precious experiences of living: to have been kidnapped by some worry or striving and then suddenly to be gracefully returned home to the present moment and reminded of love. It is almost always an occasion for the giggles.

> (Gerald May, *The Awakened Heart*)

Young people, as well as adults, have no presumptions about receiving anyone's full attention. They are formed in a world that expects and rewards distraction. They assume when the phone rings that the caller is simultaneously driving a car, playing a computer game, or standing at a cash register. They are trained to believe that a successful person is the person who can divide their attention among the largest number of activities. To be seen, heard and fully attended to by another is wishful dreaming. People are too busy. Life is too hectic. There are too many tasks to be accomplished, goals to be achieved, and diversions to be experienced.

And we have to admit that being present to a young person – or any person for that matter – *is* incredibly difficult. We too have been formed in a society that demands multi-tasking. We too grew up doing homework in front of chattering television sets and blaring stereos. We too have been trained to lift up efficiency, instead of relationship, as the highest value in ministry. Furthermore, many of us who work with teenagers have been successful because we're so good at multi-tasking! We're people with high energy who can make arrangements for a ski retreat and plan a Bible study all while driving to pick up pizza for Sunday school class. No one expects us to be fully present to kids, least of all the church. We continually receive the message that parents, church board members and pastors are happy as long as we produce as many programmes in as few hours as possible. I've counselled and talked with many youth directors and church volunteers who have been let go from their youth ministry responsibilities. None of them were dismissed for not being present to kids. Most were let go because they weren't increasing the number of kids and programmes within the church.

In a society that increasingly seeks to fracture our attention, contemplative presence becomes an act of rebellion. It's a radical in-breaking of the Holy Spirit every time we seek to be prayerfully present to another human being. However, just as we must continually return again and again to contemplative prayer in order to keep our hearts open and attentive to the presence of God, so too must we intentionally cultivate contemplative presence with young people.

Being contemplatively present to young people is often an experience of forgetting and remembering. Over and over, I forget that the souls of young people are not in my hands. I have to remember that I'm not the centre of the world. I forget that these young people are more in need of my presence than my knowledge. I have to remember that my presence and trust in God is enough. Jesus knew that forgetting can be a primary problem for those who seek to live the Christian life. His last words, as recorded in the book of Matthew, are '*Remember*, I am with you always, to the end of the age' (Matthew 28.20).

Being present to God amidst young people and being present to young people amidst God takes practice. It takes practice to remember you're not alone. It takes practice to remember that God is present and available within our relationships with kids. It takes practice to receive young people with the eyes, ears and heart of Jesus. In this chapter you will find a few of the ways I've sought to remember. These are exercises and practices I've explored to remind me of God's nearness and my desire to be open and receptive to young people.

The only Jesus you'll ever know

My first son, Noah, was born while I was a graduate student in seminary. I was working on a master's degree in Christian spirituality and spent most days listening to lectures and most nights absorbed in reading great mystical texts. Soon after Noah was born I took him to a seminary chapel service. After the service ended, I encountered one of my mentors, Sister Elizabeth Liebert, who serves as Professor of Spiritual Life at San Francisco Theological Seminary. She is a wise and prayerful teacher, and a primary reason I decided to study Christian spirituality. Beth was elated to see my new son. I let her hold him, and she gazed in delight at his face, commenting on his dark eyes and little bow mouth. She placed her finger on his head and made the sign of the cross, blessed him, and then handed him back to me and said, 'This is your greatest teacher, Mark. Treat him as such.' She looked at me while her words sank in and then walked off.

As these words took hold, I found myself looking at Noah with new eyes. This little helpless child who depended on his mother and me for care was my greatest teacher. I began to gaze on Noah with a new sense of expectation. Instead of attending to him as a series of needs that required attention, I began to be more open and receptive. I would watch him, wondering what gift he was seeking to give me, what insight he might offer, what 'lesson' this teacher sought to impart. I began to see my time with Noah as sacred. During the night hours I would wake up to his cry and think of the monks at the local monastery where I spent retreats; they too were waking throughout the night to sing and pray and attend to the presence of Christ. Over time these midnight walks with Noah became times of prayer, times of receiving God's love and insight. I tried to attend to Noah as if I were holding the baby Jesus himself, in wonder and anticipation.

When I first began training to become a youth minister there was a phrase commonly used in books and workshops to highlight the importance of our behaviour towards youth: 'You may be the only Jesus they'll ever know.' This statement was intended to stress how important it is for youth workers to pay special attention to their behaviour toward and among young people because they are representing Christ to those teenagers. I agree that we ministers need to be reminded that we seek to embody the same spirit of love and hospitality that Jesus embodied. As followers of Jesus we seek to have the 'mind of Christ' and disclose God's life in the world just as Jesus did. However, there's a way in which this idea of 'being Jesus' for the young people in our lives can warp our relationships by putting too much emphasis on *us*. When we seek to *be* Jesus we become the centre of attention – we're the ones who act, teach, heal and lead. As 'Jesus', we can't help but feel like the spotlight is on us. This creates undue pressure and can actually keep us from embodying the kind of patience and generosity of spirit Jesus embodied.

Over the years I've found it much more helpful to follow the advice of Sister Liebert and seek to treat each young person as a teacher from God, as someone God has placed in my life in order to help me grow in faith. When I encounter a young person, I find it much more helpful to think that she or he may be the only Jesus *I'll* ever know. Perhaps by seeking to encounter the presence of

Christ in young people we'll find ourselves better able to see them, hear them, feel compassion for them, and respond in kindness. Certainly Jesus encouraged us to see and treat others in this way. In the Gospel of Matthew, Jesus says God's kingdom will be inherited by those who brought him food when he was hungry, drink when he was thirsty, clothed him when naked, cared for him when sick, and visited him while he was imprisoned. When the righteous can't remember when they did these actions for Jesus, he tells them, 'Truly I tell you, just as you did it to one of the least of these who are members of my family, you did it to me' (Matthew 25.40).

Jesus does not align himself with the givers of care, he identifies with 'the least of these'. That's where his presence is to be found. Before your next encounter with young people, pause for a few minutes and pray that God will help you receive each young person as if he or she were Jesus. Close your eyes and picture their faces; ask God to remind you that each of these young people was created in the image of God. Then as you're with these teenagers, see if you can receive them in the same way that the elders of the Jewish temple received young Jesus when he came barging in, having just left his family. See if you can listen and visit with them in wonder and amazement.

Like Jesus, young people can fill us with doubt and questions. Like Jesus, they can unearth broken and unfinished places within us. Like Jesus, they can bring us to the edge of our capacities to love and forgive . . . and then demand more. Can we see that maybe the reason God has drawn us into ministry with young people isn't because we have something to offer, but because there is something we need to receive? Maybe God gathers those 13-year-olds into your Sunday school classroom because it's the only place God can get your attention. Because for some reason you're more pliable in a junior high Sunday school class, God can get your attention among these young ones, shake you up, and offer you a word of healing. Maybe youth ministry is your spiritual discipline. It's not just a place where you serve, it's a place where you are being transformed, healed, and made new. Can you see it this way? Try interacting with young people as if they are instrumental to your own freedom and healing.

The interior glance

Another way in which we might remember God's constant presence within our interactions with young people is to practise the 'interior glance' of Brother Lawrence. A Carmelite lay-brother, Brother Lawrence was neither a scholar, teacher nor skilled worker within his community. He spent most of his days working in the kitchen – and even there he proved to be clumsy and at times quite incompetent. But Brother Lawrence was a person who knew how to love well. He knew how to live in deep communion with God and with great compassion for others. He's remembered to this day for the simple way in which he dwelt within the presence of God and showered care on those he encountered. He found a way to illuminate the mundane activities of life with an abiding awareness of God's presence that he called 'practising the presence of God'.

One of the ways Brother Lawrence achieved this sense of God's presence within his normal activities was by simply glancing 'God-ward' throughout the day. These interior glances came as unplanned, unforced moments when he would remember God's presence and simply turn his heart's attention to God, opening to God in the midst of doing dishes, cleaning floors or conversing with others.

I have three children who are often with me when I'm in public places or out running errands. Sometimes when I'm grocery shopping or chatting with a friend, my kids will wander off. But no matter how engaged I am in an activity or conversation, I still have an ongoing awareness of the presence of my children. There's this sixth sense that attends to them, listens for them, notices when they're in need. Even when I'm deeply engaged in conversation, my head will turn suddenly (before I even know why) just before one of my kids jumps off a shopping cart or pulls down a carton of eggs. As a parent I know the experience of practising the presence of my children while engaged in other activities. In a similar way we can attend to the presence of God while relating to young people. We seek to keep the heart's eye on God, noticing God's expansive presence within all of our interactions with youth.

There are different ways we can remind ourselves to look toward God during our encounters with youth. First of all, we can pray, asking God to remind us of God. This is a helpful prayer to say before we encounter young people. Whether they are returning home for school, waiting in a church classroom, or walking toward us on a sidewalk, we can take a moment to breathe a simple prayer asking God to remind us of God's presence as we relate to young people.

Brother Lawrence took advantage of the little spaces within a day to remind himself of God's abiding love. We can do the same. No matter how busy we are, there are always little pauses, spaces within our day that we can use as reminders to pray and notice God. I've found that these spaces exist even within a busy youth event or church class. There are still little breaks during which I can take a breath and turn my attention toward God – sitting alone in the youth room waiting for the kids to arrive, walking to the kitchen to get snacks for Sunday school, during the few seconds of silence before the kids begin the closing prayer, waiting in my car to give a young person a ride to school. There are many of these moments within our interactions with young people that we can use to intentionally remind ourselves to stop and receive the Holy Spirit.

I've also used images and sounds as reminders to glance Godward. For eight years I lived next to a seminary that sounded chapel bells every hour. Every time I noticed the sound of the bells, I would simply enlarge my awareness, seeking to notice God. We can do the same in our ministries, allowing the sound of the front door, the water tap in the sink, or the voices of young people to remind us of God's presence. We can use images like smiles, eyes, bookbags or baseball caps to remind us to notice God. I've even drawn a cross on my hand to remind myself to notice God within my activities with youth. Every time I noticed the cross, I allowed my heart to rest in the awareness that God was present.

Over time I've noticed that these interior glances keep me in my heart. They keep me attentive to God and remind me of my desire to be hospitable toward young people. I find myself more and more aware of God's presence (or at least my desire for God's presence) within my daily life and interactions with young people. I've found that even when I forget to remember God, God prods my heart, reminding me to look and see that I'm not alone, that God's love is present and available.

The awareness examen

Another historic Christian prayer that can help expand our presence with young people is the 'awareness examen' or the 'examination of conscience'. The examen was part of a series of spiritual exercises Ignatius of Loyola discovered through his own spiritual conversion. The spiritual exercises of Ignatius became the founding formational experience for the Jesuits and are used widely today by all walks of Christians for spiritual growth and discernment.[14] Of all of the practices and exercises he employed within the Jesuit community, Ignatius felt the examen was the most essential.

Over my eight years of consulting with churches from across the country, I've found the examen to be a powerful practice for helping youth workers, parents and congregations become more aware of the Holy Spirit and more present to young people. The examen invites us to spend some time looking back over our encounters with young people, noting when we were most open and loving toward God and youth, and when we were 'forgetful' or closed to God's love. Just as you might lie in bed at night considering the experiences of your day, this prayer asks you to review a particular encounter with young people and prayerfully ask two questions:[15]

> For what moment am I most grateful?
> For what moment am I least grateful?

These two questions, prayerfully invited, help us to identify moments of consolation and desolation. *Consolation* is a classical term used over the centuries by praying Christians to identify moments when we are more open to God, ourselves and others. These are moments of life, moments of connection, moments when we feel more alive, more transparent to God and more loving toward other people. *Desolation* refers to the opposite experience – disconnection, depletion, alienation, a sense of being blocked to the presence of God, others or ourselves. By paying attention to these two moments in our lives, we become more aware of the revelatory nature of our experience. Sometimes we notice patterns or occasions when we are in the flow of God's love; other times we see moments when we seem to be caught, bound up within our own wounds and blindness.

After an activity or encounter with young people, I have found it helpful to look back and notice all the moments of gratitude, moments when I was open and receptive to God. Then I go back and notice the moments of least gratitude, moments when I was blocked in some way to the presence of God and young people. Over time, as I have reflected on these consolations and desolations, I have found that I have become better attuned to the movement of the Holy Spirit within my ministry and better able to be my true self with kids.

Take a moment to set aside your reading and experience the prayer of examen. Find a place where you can pray without interruption. Light a candle to focus your attention and remind yourself of God's presence. Then spend a few moments in silence, allowing yourself to become aware of God's presence and care for you. When you're ready, ask the Holy Spirit to go with you as you review your last encounter with young people. It might be a formal activity like Sunday school or youth group or an informal interaction with youth within your family or community. As you look over your experience let the following question arise: For what moment am I most grateful? Allow little things to emerge: a smile, a greeting, a kind word, the sunlight in the room, an engaging conversation. Then stay with whatever moment God seems to give you. Don't force anything, just be open and let the moment arise that seems to hold the most gratitude.

Let all else fall away as you spend a few moments just holding this experience of gratitude. What did the experience feel like? What were you like? What were the young people like in this experience? What might God be seeking to teach you through this experience? You might want to journal some of these insights.

Now go back over your experience with young people and this

time ask: For what moment am I least grateful? Again, just allow God to bring your attention to whatever moment seemed most filled with desolation. Take a few minutes to prayerfully journal what you have noticed.

*   *   *

In one church in which I volunteered with the youth ministry, a group of adults would engage in the awareness examen after each gathering with the high school youth group. Over time we noticed that greeting the kids as they arrived at the church continually showed up as a 'gratitude'. For some reason, just saying 'Hello' and welcoming the kids into the building was a moment when we felt more transparent to God's presence and more real and authentic toward the youth. We began to discuss what this meant. We went through Scripture and noticed the hospitality of Jesus. Over time we sensed a call to extend this greeting time. There were eight adults in the ministry at that time, and we decided that each young person who entered the church would be greeted by each one of us. We would each take a moment to approach the young person, call him or her by name, chat a bit, and in some appropriate way make physical contact – a handshake, a pat on the back, a hug. Six months later the greeting time had extended to almost 20 minutes. To this day I'm convinced many of those kids came to that church just so they could walk through the door and see eight adults call out their name, touch their hand, and beam at them with love. It was the awareness examen and our noticing of the power of the greeting time that pointed us in this direction.

I received an e-mail from Tim, a youth worker who began to practise the awareness examen after each youth group gathering. He relayed the following experience:

> During youth gatherings I would lead the kids in games, singing and Bible study. As I spent time praying the examen I noticed that the moments of desolation always occurred during the singing. This surprised me, since I love to play guitar and Christian music was integral to my own faith

formation. And yet, time after time group singing showed up as a moment of 'least gratitude'. When the time came for singing at the next youth meeting, I decided to first stop and ask the young people if they enjoyed singing. It became quiet at first, then one young woman blurted out, 'Well, it seems like this really isn't a time when we're all singing.' She hesitated, then continued, 'It seems like you're performing. Like you're having a great time singing these songs and we're suppose to listen to you . . . instead of sing along.' I was shocked and embarrassed at first, but then realized the truth of what had been said. From that point on I invited other kids to bring instruments and help plan the music and together lead singing. I'm grateful the examen helped me notice this place of disconnection. Now I feel I've been able to create something with the kids that feels much closer to what God wants for us.

While I was in seminary, I served as the volunteer youth director for a local Presbyterian church. Although the church and seminary were in an upper-middle class neighbourhood, after a few years the youth ministry began to attract a number of underprivileged kids. These students were often rough in appearance and sometimes in behaviour. Some of them were separated from their parents and living in foster homes. Others lived in government housing and had parents struggling to survive. A few of these kids had been in trouble with the law or suspended from school. After youth meetings the other leaders and I would discuss our anxiety at the influx of these kids who often were disruptive and needy. Our conversations were frequently filled with concern about how to address the behaviour of these 'rough' kids.

Then we would pray the examen over our meeting. Time after time we'd discover that the presence of these 'troubled' kids was our greatest consolation. Somehow their presence made the ministry more relevant, less frivolous. We noticed that many of the other kids from wealthier backgrounds were inundated with activities – for them youth group was just 'one more thing'. On the other hand, these new kids, even though they could be disruptive, were deeply invested in the group. They engaged wholeheartedly in discussions, prayed fervently, and soaked up attention from the ministry leadership. Instead of identifying these kids as trouble-makers, we began to see them as a sign that Jesus was present in our group. Since Jesus always attracted the poor and marginal-ized, we began to pray that we might become a ministry that attracted even more of these 'discarded' kids who had few places where they felt welcomed.

Returning home

Every time we remember God's presence, every time we remem-ber to act from our true selves, every time we're reminded to open and receive a young person, we experience a little homecoming. Meister Eckhart once said, 'God is at home, it's we who've gone out for a walk.' These exercises remind us to look homeward, to turn and notice that the kingdom of God is among us (and within us).[16]

As we seek to live within the awareness of God, we often dis-cover patterns of forgetfulness. We notice addictions to activity, reactions to particular kids who make us feel anxious or angry. When we allow God to expand our awareness, we not only become aware of God's presence and our capacity to love, we also become more aware of our brokenness and propensity to shut God out. These sometimes painful noticings can also be useful. They can help us see the ways we are still in need of healing. They can help point out our resistances to God or particular young people. It's helpful to notice the places within us that are needy, resistant or unfinished. We can bring a gentle compassion to these aspects of ourselves, asking God to heal these broken or wounded places so we might become more authentic in our lives and our ministry with young people.

Seeking to expand our presence to God and young people can be a trying endeavour. We need to give ourselves permission to try a variety of exercises that help remind us of God's life among us. Sometimes we'll discover a particular exercise, a sound or image, that helps us abide in Christ throughout our encounters with youth. Then we may find ourselves forgetting for weeks on end, caught up in our own activity and sense of importance. Or we may find ourselves stuck and notice that a particular exercise isn't bearing fruit. And so we begin again. We try something else. We turn to God once more and pray, 'Help me to remember you within this ministry.' And then we trust. We forget again. We pray. We try again. And over time there begins to be a shift. We notice ourselves remembering, more often than before, that we're not alone, that the ministry is being carried, that there is rest even in the most stressful of situations, because Jesus is both beside us and before us, making a way.

9

Forming the beloved community

—————➤◆◄—————

A contemplative approach to youth ministry has been for me a rediscovery of community. I've learned to no longer do youth ministry alone. Before this I had always convinced myself it was easier to do things by myself – and to a certain extent, some of it is easier alone. However, the easier way or the quicker way is most definitely NOT the better way. In taking the very slow road of community and listening to one another's pain and joy . . . each person's story . . . we get to a safe place where each is valued and we can work together in mutual support seeking out the unique gifts each person brings to the table. Our youth have truly resonated to this reality.

> (Chris Berthelsen, pastor, First Lutheran Church,
> St Paul, Minnesota)

One cannot be concerned about the spirituality of teens without being at the same time concerned about the spiritu-ality of the entire community . . . the message embodied in a community's WAY is more powerful than any message in a textbook or on a blackboard. And is not this the problem that persons dealing with youth have been encountering again and again in recent years: finding a community that will embody the gospel in such a way that young people can recognize the presence of Jesus?

> (Michael Warren, *Youth and the Future of the Church*)

No matter how earnest our desire to pray and be present to youth, our ministries will be short-lived if they aren't grounded in rela-tionships with other Christians. It takes a greenhouse to nurture the souls of young people; a greenhouse formed by adults who want to know God. A young person's faith is best tended by a variety of relationships within a Christian community. And yet, sadly, youth ministry is one of the most isolated ministries within the Church. If we seek to form a contemplative youth ministry, the participation of the wider church community is essential.

Dietrich Bonhoeffer wrote that there is no such thing as an individual Christian. If we seek to share the life of Jesus with young people, we can't do it alone. Christians believe it's only as we gather together that we truly embody the Spirit of Jesus. Together we become his eyes, hands, mind and heart.

A friend of mine from the Claremont School of Theology once interviewed a group of pastors from Southern California. These pastors were diverse in their denominational, racial, ethnic and theological backgrounds. They led churches that varied in size, practice and congregational make-up. Yet when my friend asked these pastors what kind of youth minister they wanted for their churches, the answer was the same: a twenty-something, attractive, guitar-playing, charismatic, youth-savvy, hip, hard-working, van-driving, free-spirited, denominationally loyal, Jesus-loving, Bible-carrying, old-people-friendly, faith-filled, fiscally responsible youth leader (preferably male with decorative facial hair, and mountain bike strapped to car roof – OR, if unavailable, a spunky, to-die-for, fashion-conscious female who will cry once on youth Sundays and twice on summer mission trips).

These Southern California pastors, and almost every church I know, secretly prays and waits for the coming of the youth ministry messiah. That dynamo of a young adult who can relieve parents and church members of their burdensome youth, take away all the anxiety over the junior high Sunday school class, and offer forgiveness to church members saying, 'Come to me all you who are heavy burdened and I will give you rest. Your ridiculous attempts at ministry are washed away and forgotten. I release you from all guilt and responsibility. I, the saviour to adolescents, am all that is needed. Go now in peace and worry not for your children, for they are safe in my tanned and well-defined arms.'

Like the Israelites who grew tiresome of attending to the mystery of God's presence in their midst, our churches shout and pray to the Lord, 'Give us a king! A leader! Or at least someone who can decipher hip-hop lyrics!' We adults see the television images. We see the new fashions. We understand there are new forms of music and technologies. And we know we are hopelessly un-cool. We still own eight-track tapes. Our clothing style is circa 1985. Our roller skates have two rows of wheels. There's no way young people will think we have anything to do with The Lord, Our God – especially when we look more like a disciple of The Wal-Mart, Our Discount Store. And yet, didn't Jesus gather together an ordinary, uneducated, un-cool working-class group of fishermen to help awaken the world to the love of God? There are youth ministers who are incredibly gifted in communicating the gospel to young people, but if these youth ministers don't have a group of Christians committed to serving alongside them, they will soon burn out.

Ministry of the beloved community

No matter how faithfully we pray and befriend young people, no matter how young, hip, capable or 'contemplative' we become, if we would follow Jesus, we cannot minister to kids alone. I have watched numerous well-meaning parents, youth ministry volunteers and paid professionals quickly burn out after seeking to share faith with youth by themselves. The energy of young people, the suffering of families, the odd hours, the isolation from the rest of the adults, the enormous task of passing on the intimacies of our faith to young people – all of these factors and more are too heavy for any one person to bear without shutting down or treating the youth as projects.

In youth ministry circles we often forget that ministry is to be done with others. We forget that Moses was given a community of elders to help lead the people of Israel. We forget that Jesus began his ministry by gathering Andrew and Simon Peter and the rest of the disciples. We overlook the fact that Paul and the other earliest missionaries in the New Testament almost always travelled in twos when they went to share the gospel. How can we teach young people that the Christian faith is about community when we're often alone in our ministry? How can we ask youth to break out of their cliques and befriend other students when they see us often isolated from other adults? How can we ask them to open up and share their experiences of life with one another, when they notice that we don't have a peer group of our own who share our faith and life struggles?

A ministry done with others is a ministry of presence. Jesus tells us, 'Where two or three are gathered in my name, I am there among them' (Matthew 18.20). Jesus reminds us that if we are to reveal the reality of God, we must minister grounded in relationship. When we minister together, Jesus assures us that he is there – present and moving among us. If our ministries seek to communicate the nearness of God, we can't just rely on our own solitary contemplative practice; we must practise our prayer within a community that shares a calling to befriend young people.

A communal ministry not only bears the presence of Christ, it also allows for greater relationships with young people. I consider myself a very 'youth-friendly' type of guy. I've spent lots of time with teenagers and have discovered I can relate to many different types of young people. However, no matter how well I listen, no matter how friendly or funny I am, there are many kids who just don't 'connect' with me – as well as a significant group of kids who just plain don't like me. When we minister with others, young people are presented with a diversity of relationships within the beloved community. A young person befriended by a middle-aged receptionist, a 20-year-old college student, a retired bank manager, and a young parent of a toddler – all who seek to live and share the Christian life – will have a much richer image of Jesus, a wider understanding of Christian community, and more encouraging sense of her own place in God's family than if she were ministered to by one person.

When we minister with young people together, we share the burdens of ministry. There are more of us to divide the work of teaching, befriending, organizing outings and praying for kids. In my first four years of youth ministry at a fairly typical suburban church, I was overwhelmed by the issues young people brought to me: divorce, custody battles, sexual abuse, self-mutilation, suicidal thoughts, issues of sexual identity, questions about vocation – and I haven't even mentioned the spiritual questions I encountered! I wouldn't have been able to respond to most of these issues if I hadn't gathered other adults to minister alongside me.

Deeper still, when we minister together, we are able to better discern and follow the movement of the Holy Spirit. Discernment refers to 'testing the spirits' – the process of sifting, weighing and distinguishing what is of God and what is not. Discernment is about locating and staying close to the presence of Jesus. Discernment is about drawing close to God, locating ourselves in God, and then seeing how the Spirit is drawing us to live and act. Discernment is critical to the Christian life and ministry. And yet, to discern we need others. It is in community that we hear God most clearly. Each of us has gaps in our spiritual hearing; we need others to help us notice when we've gone deaf or are drowning out God.

Finally, it's in community that we become our true selves. Young people are hungry for authentic relationships with adults, yet it is incredibly difficult for ministers and adults to be authentic among young people. When we engage young people in ministry, we often want to be a role model, we want to project a faith life that has eliminated all doubts. We want to offer kids an endless well of time, energy and compassion. These desires and projections come not only from us, they emanate also from our churches and from young people themselves. It often seems everyone expects us to be super-human in our relationships with kids.

We need to minister in community so we can become real, so we can touch the ground and be reminded of our frailty. It is neither healthy nor biblical to minister without a group of people who can listen to our doubts, point out our shortcomings, and remind us of our belovedness in God. There are many times when it's appropriate to hold back some of our personal lives from the young people we serve; however, I've found that if I don't have a group of people who are committed to sharing my life, I become more and more distant in my relationships with teenagers and God.

There are countless other reasons why Jesus asks us to minister in community – so we might help one another resist the violent hyperactivity of the culture, so we might carry one another's burdens, and so we might have greater wisdom in accompanying young people. But the primary question for many of us who minister with youth isn't about the value of ministering with others, it's about how to *find* a community of people who are willing to minister with youth. Today's young people are being abandoned by adults in way no previous generation has ever experienced. Consider these words from sociologist Christian Smith in his thorough study on the spiritual and religious lives of teens:

> Significant numbers of teens today live their lives with little but the most distant adult direction and oversight. They spend the greater part of most weekdays in schools surrounded almost exclusively by their peers. Their parents are working and otherwise busy. Members of their extended family live in distant cities. Their teachers are largely preoccupied with discipline, classroom instruction and grading. Their neighbors tend to stay out of each other's business. These teens may have their own cars, cell phones, spending money, and televisions in their bedrooms. Or they may simply spend all their free time hanging out with friends and associates at the mall, on the streets, at friends' houses, or other places away from home. In any case, when school lets out, it may be hours before a parent gets home from work. If a teen works, his or her co-workers are mostly other teenagers who are also flipping burgers or working cash registers; their supervisors may be adults, but few teens have significant relationships with them beyond taking orders and collecting paychecks.[17]

There are few adults who have the time and willingness to be with young people, even their own teenagers. It's no different within the Church. In my experience, most churches are desperate to find people willing to minister with youth. Most adults and church members have been convinced that only the cool, the young or the ignorant would dare enter a room full of 13-year-olds and teach them a faith that has been passed down for 2,000 years.

In contemplative youth ministry we're not just recruiting chaperones, we're seeking to form a group of people who will serve in the youth ministry as a 'covenant community'. We are looking for people who will see the ministry as part of their own spiritual growth. Just as a group of adults might gather within a church to pray or study the Bible, in contemplative youth ministry an adult community is gathered that prays, shares their lives together, and serves the youth of their community.

Gathering a covenant community

In my work to integrate prayer and relationship within youth ministry, I have developed a calling process for gathering adults to accompany young people on their journeys in faith. This process draws on a community's patience and trust in God. Over the past ten years I've seen this calling process help bring together youth ministry teams that pray, discern, deepen relationships and serve together. These 'covenant communities' tend the Spirit, keeping the sacred dimension of the Christian faith alive and available to young people. I've watched as youth ministries previously involving one or two adults grow to 18 to 20 adult volunteers as a result of this process – not because there's any magic, but because adults aren't expected to be chaperones but instead are treated as spiritual seekers – people who need prayer and friendship as much as young people. Adults aren't simply asked to drive vans or read from a curriculum manual, they are asked to serve within a community of people who meet weekly for prayer, faith sharing and discernment – as well as ministry with youth (these meetings will be discussed further in Chapter 10).

How do we gather together adults? The following calling process was developed in order to gather a community of people who sense a call to share the way of Jesus with young people. The following process is a discernment approach to volunteer recruitment. Although originally designed and tested for use in congregation-based youth ministries, this process may be found useful within a variety of ministry settings. The heart of this process is listening. Pastoral leaders, congregations and individual members are asked to listen prayerfully to whom the Spirit of God is calling within their community to accompany young people on the Way of Jesus.

Before you invite people to minister with young people, it's important to remember that you're seeking people who have a sense of call to this ministry. You're not just looking for a warm body, you're seeking people with an interior sense that their participation in this ministry is intimately connected to how God is moving within their life. Make sure that you recruit among the diverse groups within your congregation. Be open to elderly people, parents and even youth serving in this ministry. Be open to whomever God may call to serve.

Seek to embody a sense of trust as you engage in this process. Trust God and trust your congregation. Most recruitment within churches has a sense of urgency and desperation. For example, read the recruitment announcement that recently ran in the newsletter from a local church:

WE NEED HELP!

Fall is just around the corner and we still have nobody to teach our Middle School Sunday school class.

IF WE DON'T HAVE A TEACHER BY AUGUST 20TH WE WILL BE FORCED TO CANCEL THE CLASS.

Call the church office if you or someone you know can do this important task!

It almost makes you want to run . . . far away. An announcement this desperate is frightening – causing any and all who read it to think the middle school students must be one terrible bunch of kids. What's sad is that someone will probably respond to this announcement out of guilt ('I didn't want the class to be cancelled!') and then carry resentment that they got 'stuck' with serving.

A contemplative approach to recruitment rests on trust. We trust that God will raise the people we need for the ministry. If not, then maybe our church isn't called to youth ministry. Maybe our kids should attend the ministry next door or participate in the church in another way. We trust that the youth ministry is God's ministry; that God seeks to disciple young people; that God will lead, guide and provide for this ministry.

We also trust our congregation. There's no need to rely on tricks, manipulation or guilt to force people into serving youth.

God will call the people to serve. And when they're called, we trust they will be the right people – even if they're not the people we'd choose. As I've practised this calling process in a variety of churches, I am amazed at the variety of adults who felt drawn to serve within the youth ministry. I have had churches that developed teams of eight to ten adults that were all over 50 years of age. I've seen some teams made up solely of parents and other ministry teams that had people aged from 14 to 83.

Not only do we trust in this process, we also commit to listening. As we seek to gather together a ministry community, we listen with our hearts to the nudges and stirrings of the Spirit. Who is God calling to this ministry? How is the Spirit working among us? We listen to people without expectations, pre-judgement or anxiety. We seek to hear within each person we encounter the unique way in which God is moving and calling.

Finally, this process requires a commitment to prayer. At regular intervals within our recruitment, we make space and time to direct our attention to God. Again and again we turn to God. What is it we want in this process? What is it that God wants in this process? We take our attention off ourselves and our own expectations and turn to God saying, 'Your will be done . . .'

The calling process

The following steps outline a process for inviting the church community's involvement in youth ministry.

Facilitators

A minimum of two people should work together to call people to serve in the youth ministry. Preferably not two staff members, but two people who seek to support and nurture the congregation's ministry with youth. Jesus always sent people out in twos. This keeps the burden and focus off of any one particular individual.

Prayer and planning

Once the two (or more) facilitators have been selected, they should begin their first meeting in prayer. This prayer should be a reminder that the focus of this process is not on them. Their role in this work is not to be successful, but simply to be faithful to what the Spirit is doing within their community. It's good to lead a prayer that goes something like:

> God, this is your church, your ministry. These are your young people. Help us listen for how you are at work in our community. Help us not to be manipulative or anxious but to trust you as we seek to gather a community of people to serve in this ministry. Help us to be faithful to how you are calling us to serve in this process. Finally, we ask you to guide us in discovering the people you are seeking to raise up for this ministry. We pray all these things in Jesus' name. Amen.

Listening to the community

The first task of the facilitators is to talk with as many people as possible within the congregation. These conversations can take place in informal settings such as coffee-hour or more formal settings such as board meetings. The goal of this stage is for the facilitators to ask as many as possible within the congregation the following question: *Who would you name within this congregation as someone who enjoys young people and would serve as a good volunteer within the youth ministry?* It's important to invite people to think beyond age and social categories. Just because a person is retired, in high school, a parent, or has irregular church attendance, doesn't mean he or she isn't called to this ministry.

Often people will respond something like, 'Margie always tithes to the youth programme, but she is 80 years old and I don't know if she has the energy for ministry with young people.' Or, 'Chloe is good with kids, but she has two teens of her own and I don't think it would be good for her to be involved in the ministry if her kids are in it.' Or, 'Tom would be ideal . . . but I don't know about his commitment to ministry. He only shows up at church two or three times a year, and mostly spends time coaching the swim team.' The rule at this stage of the process is to write down every name that is offered – no matter what qualifiers or misgivings are attached to that name. We don't know who God is calling into this ministry, so we have to be open to all names given.

As the facilitators circulate this question throughout the

congregation they will begin to collect a list of names. Continue collecting names until you have spoken to most of the congregation. Avoid blanket recruitment announcements in newsletters or bulletins. It's important to make this process personal. Spend the time talking to people – God is in relationships, so make contact with people and let them in on the discerning. Remember that it's an honour to serve in youth ministry – people who serve in youth ministry have the sacred task of passing on the intimacies of our faith to the next generation. You don't want just anybody to serve, you want people who are called.

Meeting with the pastor

After the facilitators have gathered names they should meet with the senior pastor. The pastor should look over the names of people listed and advise the facilitators of any names that should be removed from the list. (Pastors are often privy to information about church members that might be important when calling people to work with youth.)

Praying over the names

It's important to spend some time praying over those who are named. Keep God at the centre of this process by regularly praying for the people drawn to this ministry. Facilitators might pray something like:

> Holy God, help us to be faithful to you. Help us listen for the people you are calling into this ministry. This is your church, this is your ministry, these are your young people. Help us listen and be faithful to the tasks you have given us. We pray for each of the people who have been named. We ask that you speak clearly to those you have called into this ministry. Help them discern the ways in which you are asking them to serve. Help us not to be manipulative but to be open and grateful as we speak with them. We trust you, and thank you for trusting us with your work. We pray all these things in Jesus' name. Amen.

Setting appointments with potential volunteers

The facilitators then contact those people named by the community as potential volunteers for the ministry, beginning with any people who were named more than once by the congregation. Make personal appointments with each of the people named on the list. This takes time because often you must co-ordinate three or more schedules. Again, we want to honour the people named so we seek to meet them in person. The invitation to serve should not be left on an answering machine or given in a hallway conversation. We are asking people to discern a call to ministry; this call needs to be honoured with time and space.

Meeting with potential volunteers

Two facilitators should meet together with each potential volunteer, preferably in a home or other environment that allows for personal conversation. Again, it's good for the facilitators to get together a few minutes before meeting with a potential volunteer to pray and prepare for the meeting.

Presenting the invitation

Facilitators should explain to each potential volunteer that he or she has been named by the congregation as someone who has gifts in ministering with young people. Potential volunteers should understand that they are being asked to discern (to listen if God is calling them) into the youth ministry. Make sure you stress that the volunteer is not being asked to be a chaperone or an 'answer person' but is being asked to engage in the youth ministry as a setting for their own spiritual growth. Facilitators should mention that the volunteer would be expected to be part of a community of volunteers who will meet regularly to pray, share and discern. The time expectations should also be communicated clearly – often it's good to ask volunteers to serve for at least one year.

Meetings with potential volunteers should be relaxed and informal. Take the pressure off the meeting by encouraging people to say 'No' if they feel uncomfortable or unable to accept the invitation for any reason. Trust that God will provide people for the ministry. Avoid using guilt or manipulation ('The kids totally love you. It will be such a disappointment if you don't participate . . .').

Don't ask people for an answer at this initial meeting. Potential volunteers should be encouraged to pray about their call and discuss it with their family (especially if they are a parent of a teenager). Give people at least a week to pray and think it over before you contact them to hear their response. Of course, spend time praying for folks as you give them time to discern. After a week or so contact people either in person or by phone and listen to their response. Trust that each person is responding to his or her sense of God's call.

Modifying the call

Often people will respond with a variety of modifications to the original invitation to serve in the ministry: 'I can't help out every week but I could volunteer *every other* week.' 'Would it be OK to just volunteer for larger events like mission trips?' 'I'd be glad to help fix meals or drive, but I can't make a regular commitment to be part of the ministry team.'

All such responses should be considered. Usually it's best to try and receive whatever time and energies people offer – as long as the facilitators make sure there is a critical mass of four to eight people who have said 'Yes' to serving as part of a regular ministry community.

Advocates

Often there are people who are supportive of the ministry but don't feel called to work directly with young people. Perhaps they are elderly, have a child in the youth group, or have some other reason that prevents them from working with the youth. I've found these people can be very valuable to the ministry as 'advocates'.

Advocates are part of the ministry community, although they don't actually work with the youth. They attend youth leader meetings. They pray, discern and even help plan with the youth ministry, but aren't expected to engage in the youth activities. Advocates can help to remind the ministry team of the larger church context, looking for ways in which the ministry can integrate its work with the life of the church as a whole. At the same time, when advocates are among the larger congregation, they seek to remind the congregation of the activities, interests and struggles of the youth ministry. In this way advocates are bridge-builders – fostering connections between the youth ministry and the wider congregation.

Advocates can play a valuable support role within the ministry without being enmeshed in all its relationships and tasks. It's good to have at least one advocate on your team to help give the ministry an outside perspective.

Celebration

After the team has been called, there should be a gathering with everyone – volunteers, ministers, youth and facilitators – to celebrate the end of the calling process and the faithfulness of the volunteers' responses to the call.

*   *   *

Because this process asks congregations to take time for prayer, discernment and personal relationship, it is a much slower form of recruitment. Churches I've observed have taken anything from one to six months. It takes time to meet, talk, pray, listen, discern and then make decisions as to who is called into the youth ministry.

Feel free to modify the process based on the unique character of your congregation. You may want to host a meal for all potential volunteers and present the invitation to ministry to them all at once. Previous churches have held a special dinner in a home with hand-made invitations and other personal touches that communicate the respect and gratitude the church has for these potential volunteers.

Once a community of adults has been called to ministry, it's good to start with a retreat where people can pray together, get to know one another and talk about the way in which they hope to serve young people. I have put suggestions for a sample volunteer retreat in Appendix 3 of this book. Every church I have worked with that has used this process has increased the number of adults within their youth ministry. Depending on the size of the church, most congregations have gathered any number from 8 to 22 volunteers. The first church I worked with using this process ended up calling 20 adults to serve weekly in the youth ministry – out of a congregation of only 150 members. Five years later 15 of these adults were still serving. Imagine the experience of young people when they engage in a youth ministry in which 8 to 20 adults pray for them, seek to be present to them and respond to their spiritual needs and questions. This is the kind of ministry Jesus established, a group of people called together to pray and serve together, to share the good news of God's presence among us.

10

The liturgy for discernment

When I think of the people who minister on our team – Lisa, Jennifer, Graham and Paul – I feel more like they're my brothers and sisters than even my own blood. I have shared things with them that I haven't even told my wife. They bear my burdens and the burdens of ministry with me. The kids see our relationships, and I think it tells them more about the Christian life than what we're teaching them during lesson times.

(Doug Ladsen, utility lineman and volunteer youth worker, Saron United Church of Christ, Linton, Indiana)

Individual perception, reasoning and understanding are always limited. Even a person who feels absolutely certain that a specific revelation comes from God may be mistaken as to how it is to be applied. Because God often reveals part of the picture to one person and another part to another person, it is prudent to consult one another to discern God's counsel, guidance and direction, even if there is no apparent reason to do so. While circumstances sometimes require us to act without consulting others, the danger of arrogance and error in proceeding on our own can be great.

(Suzanne Farnham, Joseph P. Gill, R. Taylor McLean, Susan M. Ward, *Listening Hearts*)

At 11.27 a.m. in the Myra T. Shipley Fellowship Room of First Friendly Church, youth minister Paul Lopez has the fixed smile of a professional customer service representative. It's the kind of smile that says, 'I'm politely pretending to be listening to you, while I'm really thinking of something else.' His eyes, glazed and unfocused, are pointed in the direction of Carl, a parent and youth ministry volunteer who for the third time this year is describing his college mentor.

'Now most of us assume an archaeologist would be an ace in geography. But I'm telling you, during our trip to Israel, Dr Carlton couldn't tell the hills of Jericho from a hill of beans!' [Dramatic pause] 'Did I ever tell you about what happened when we tried to find the Sea of Galilee?'

'Yes,' Paul says weakly, knowing it will have no effect.

'Well, Dr Carlton was supposed to meet me at the *northeast* shore of the Galilean Sea . . .'

Paul is not listening. Paul is thinking of the work he has to do to prepare for the weekend youth retreat. He steals a glance at his watch, realizing he will be stuck in this meeting for at least another two hours. Paul is silently praying, pleading with God, 'Please, Lord, make him stop. Don't let him tell the whole story. Lord, I'm only paid 20 hours a week to do this job . . . Please don't let two of them be wasted on this meeting.'

Margaret, the middle school Sunday school teacher, breaks in, 'Speaking of doctors, I know I said this last week, but let me say it again, there is no way I can continue to lift those chairs to set up that classroom. My back can't take it any more. I was on an 800 milligram prescription of Ibuprofen, but now the doctor thinks I need to switch to Extra Strength Tylenol. Well, my sister tried that and . . .'

A small tear rolls slowly down Paul's face. 'How long must I suffer, how long will you test my patience, Lord . . .'

Across the street at Second Church of the Lord, Polly Gilbert quickly takes her seat in the youth room. She looks at the clock on the wall. 7.01. Following a brief prayer the director of Christian education opens the meeting, 'Good morning, everyone. Before we begin I want to remind everyone to keep their reports to five minutes or less. Last week we went 15 minutes over time. Only share those items that are relevant to the whole group.' He gives a quick glance at Polly.

Polly looks at her notes and scratches out 'Mom's illness' and

'Prayers for Allison'. She sits with her head down trying to hold back her tears. *I feel so out of place . . . I don't know what I'm doing with the youth . . . My mother is back in the hospital. I still can't believe that Allison, one of our most active high school girls, has been cutting her arms . . . I'm overwhelmed . . .*

'Polly? Polly? What do we need to know from our youth ministry department?'

*   *   *

There are two primary methods for running a staff meeting. The first is what I call the 'chaos' approach. A 'chaos' meeting is open and informal. It moves and shifts based on the whims and moods of the group. The length and content of the meeting swing wildly. One week the staff is engaged in a heated two-hour discussion on cleaning supplies. The next week a volunteer parent spends 45 minutes sharing about her mother's trip to Canada. There is a 'feeling' of attending to relationships . . . yet few people are really listening. Most people are simply talking, dumping out whatever thoughts, tensions or issues they happen to be carrying that day.

In contrast to the 'chaos' meeting is the 'control' approach. Based on business models, this staff meeting is focused on efficiency and production. The meeting is more formal and structured, with everyone attending to the clock. Staff members come ready to do business, setting their personal lives aside. 'Control' meetings focus on concrete items – numbers, budgets, goals and tasks. The focus of control meetings is to get more work done faster. Personal sharing, brainstorming and open discussion are left for sub-groups.

Most congregations are somewhere in between these two approaches, containing a mix of corporate efficiency and personality-driven conversation. Youth ministry leaders are no different. Most youth ministry staffs tend to take either a chaos approach or a control approach to staff meetings. And yet neither one of these – nor the continuum that lies between them – is grounded in Christian living. New youth ministry volunteers who step into either of these meetings will quickly become disillusioned and demoralized because the centre of Christian communities should be neither personal free-for-alls nor corporate efficiency. At the centre of a ministry there should exist a spiritual community; a covenant group that is attentive to God, discerning of the Spirit, and caring for one another. In youth ministry our methods are as significant as our message. If our meetings are focused on personalities or productivity, we'll tend to measure the success of the ministry based on whether kids 'like' the youth leaders or the amount of programmes produced.

In 1997, I designed a different process for staff meetings, a process that seeks to place prayer, relationships and discernment as the primary tasks of a Christian meeting. This process has been used throughout the partner congregations within the Youth Ministry and Spirituality Project. It is a process based on prayer, relationships and deep listening.

The 'liturgy for discernment' is a form of communal discernment. The word 'liturgy' comes from the Greek word *leitourgia*, which means 'the work of the people'. In the Christian tradition this word has usually referred to worship, but it can also be understood more broadly as the way we gather in the presence of God.

Discernment is the process of listening for the voice of God. For Christians, discernment refers to 'testing the spirits' – the process of seeking and discovering what is of God and what is not (1 John 4.1ff.). Discernment is an art, a skill and a gift. It requires a desire not only to know God's call but to follow God's leading. Discernment requires humility, a willingness to set aside our own plans, agendas and aspirations (this is often referred to in the tradition as 'holy indifference') so we might be free to respond to God's bidding. We need humility in discernment, not only in relation to God, but also so we might be open to the input of others. As Christians we trust that God is most clearly heard through and in the midst of other followers of Jesus. Discernment is also mindful of Jesus. We discern in relationship to Scripture, watching how our sense of God's calling resonates with the life of Jesus.

Discernment is not a one-time event but an ongoing practice. We return again and again, constantly seeking to deepen our awareness of God's presence and calling. The hope of discernment is that over time our lives and ministries will become more transparent to God's life and more faithful to Jesus' way of love. No matter how sincere we are in our discernment, the truth is we can never be certain we are encountering God's presence or following God's call. We will never, in this life, definitively know God's call;[18] that's why we call it Christian 'faith'. And yet, over time we often look back and notice signs of God's presence and our own faithfulness.

The liturgy for discernment is a communal practice that invites us into deeper co-operation with the Spirit in the midst of the work of ministry. The liturgy was originally designed for people engaged in youth ministry, but it can also be used whenever Christians gather to do the work of God. The liturgy changes the tone and spirit in which the 'business' of ministry is done. The liturgy invites an atmosphere of prayer and listening rather than simply efficiency and productivity. In contrast to other approaches to ministry, this process emphasizes deepening relationships – with oneself, others and the Spirit of God. My experience has been that when people spend time in prayer and relationship building, the ministry becomes a great source of nourishment; people enjoy the ministry, serve with greater authenticity and stay involved longer. One church I've worked with in Oregon called 18 adults to the youth ministry. After meeting each week for seven years and engaging in the liturgy of discernment, these same 18 adults are still serving within the youth ministry. Imagine the continuity and stability the youth feel within this ministry.

The liturgy for discernment has two basic movements. In the first half of the meeting, the process moves 'inward', centring the group in relationships. Through ritual, conversation, listening and prayer, the group is reconnected with their own hearts, one another and the Spirit of God among them. These relationships are then focused around the call, or central identity, of the group. This is the pivot point of the meeting, when the group's attention moves outward, reflecting on its collective sense of identity and God's call. ('Who are we and how is God calling us?') Business items are then responded to within this deeper awareness of self, others, God and call (or group purpose). As a group practises this way of doing ministry, its members begin to operate less and less as a business committee and more and more as a spiritual community – lives are shared, relationships are built, spirits are formed and gifts are exercised.

Return to the two ministry team meetings described at the beginning of the chapter. See if you can get a sense of how these meetings might be different if they were focused on prayer, deep listening and discernment:

At 11.27 a.m. in the Myra T. Shipley Fellowship Room of First Friendly Church, youth minister Paul Lopez enters the room. The other six members of his youth ministry team have already arrived and are seated in a circle, chatting amicably. Paul smiles and greets people, then lights a candle in the middle of the group and says out loud, 'We light this candle as a reminder of Christ's light and presence here among us.' A gentle silence falls over the group. Paul takes his seat, closes his eyes, and catches his breath after a busy morning. He takes a moment to remember that God is present beneath the stress of the upcoming youth retreat. After a few minutes of silence Carl, a parent and volunteer, says, 'Lord, we've got a lot going on this week. We ask that you help us to listen to what you want us to do. Help us in our planning with these kids. They need you, Lord. And we do too. Amen.'

Paul addresses the group, 'Let's take a moment, as we do each week, and just check in. Let's each take a minute or two to tell one another how we are doing. As each of us shares, we'll ask that the rest of the group remain in silence. We want to keep from falling into conversation; just listen with care to how each person is doing today.'

There is silence for a minute or two. Then Carl shares that he just got his pictures back from Israel, and he's still overwhelmed by the whole experience. It wasn't what he expected, and yet the crowds and craziness of the whole trip has made him see the Bible in a new way.

Carl finishes and the group returns to silence. Then Margaret starts to speak. She's worried about her back. The last visit to the doctor was unsettling. It seems like no one knows what the problem is. She's worried she might have to have surgery. She feels a little depressed that she can't do the things she used to be able to do.

Margaret finishes and the group returns to silence. Then Paul shares that he feels very stressed about the upcoming retreat. One of the parent drivers cancelled last night and there aren't enough cars to get everyone to the camp. The food still hasn't been purchased, and he feels frustrated that he hasn't had time to prepare the teaching sessions for the retreat. 'I have a lot of anxiety at this meeting,' he shares, 'because I'm worried we're not going to get the preparations done in time.'

Judy, a college student, shares that her week has been pretty good. She went to the lake with some friends and had a great time. It was nice to get away from school. She's looking forward to the retreat as another chance to escape school and an opportunity to deepen her relationship with some of the sophomore girls.

When all of the sharing has ended, Paul asks Carl to lead the group in *lectio divina*. Carl reads Mark 4.35–41 – a description of Jesus and the disciples in a storm. He reads the passage three times. The group falls into silent prayer for ten minutes. Then Carl asks people to share from the prayer.

Again there is silence, then Judy begins to speak, '"Asleep on the cushion" is what stood out to me. How could Jesus be asleep on the cushion? I almost started to laugh. I mean the world is in trouble, there's a storm, everybody's freaked out, and he's sleeping. I just think there's something cool about that. It's like deep down everything is going to be OK.'

There's quiet, then Paul speaks, 'The word "awe" is what came to me. "Awe". I really want to have a sense of "awe" in my life. I feel like I spend so much time doing all these little details I never stand back and just take it all in. I could just feel that this weekend I need to take a walk outside or something and just remember to be in "awe" at Jesus.'

Others share their words and insight. After everyone has spoken, Paul says, 'OK, well, given all that we've shared, how do we sense God is calling us?' No one speaks for a minute or two. Then Margaret says, 'I'm still thinking about Judy saying she felt like laughing. I mean, the other disciples would've been really angry if you were on that boat and started laughing during the storm . . . But I think Jesus would've been right there with you, laughing alongside you. I think about our kids. Every time I go into that youth room they're horsing around and laughing. They love to laugh. I think that's why I serve in this ministry. Somehow they cheer me up and remind me of the lighter side of life.' She pauses for a moment. 'So I just think we all need to lighten up more. I think we need to go on this weekend and have fun with these kids. We need to laugh with them and let them know we trust that God is here and everything is going to be all right – even if we don't find another van driver or . . . I guess, even if the doctors can't get my medication right . . .'

The group talks about Margaret's insight for a few more minutes, and then Paul says, 'Well, let's keep these insights and our prayer in the room as we look at the work we have to do for this retreat . . .' The group then begins to look over the tasks for the upcoming retreat and makes plans. After 30 minutes or so, Paul asks Margaret to close the meeting in prayer. The group stands, holds hands, and Margaret prays: 'Resting Jesus, help us to hear your laughter this weekend. Help us to carry you, resting in our hearts as we go about the work of this ministry. And most importantly, help us to share a sense of awe and wonder with the young people. Awe and wonder at who you are. Thank you, Jesus. Amen.'

Notice the different pace of the meeting and the space given for silence, sharing and prayer. The work of the ministry was addressed, but only after the group had centred itself in prayer and relationship. This is only an example, so it appears less messy than if you were to watch a real ministry team engaged in this process. But the connections between the prayer and the group's call and the sense of moving from anxiety to a sense of peace about the work is common among the groups I've observed in this process.

Imagine Polly, in the second example at the beginning of this chapter, participating in a meeting that honoured prayer and relationship. How would Polly's sense of isolation and doubt shift if she were allowed to bring her whole self to the table? How would her vocation as a youth minister feel with the support of others who share Polly's struggles within the ministry, her suffering over her mother and her prayer for the wounded kids in the youth group?

A circle of trust[19]

The liturgy for discernment offers a process for group gatherings that is rooted in a careful listening to ourselves, one another, and the call of the Spirit. Below is a step-by-step description of the movements within the liturgy for discernment.

Ritual

As people gather to meet there is an opening ritual. This should be a simple activity that draws the group's attention to the presence of God. It could be a song, a moment of silence, or the lighting of a candle. The ritual consecrates the meeting, changing the context from ordinary time and space to sacred time and space. The ritual announces to the group, 'We are coming into an awareness of the Presence of God.' Avoid pastoral prayers or other rituals that rely on the gifts of only one person. The ritual should be repeatable no matter who is in attendance and should last no longer than a couple of minutes.

Relating

This is a time for building relationships within the community. Each member of the group is asked, 'How are you?' and is given one to two minutes to check-in. (This may seem too brief, but when there is real listening present, people tend to be more mindful of their words. A lot gets shared in a brief amount of time.) This is a time of deep listening, of attending to one another. Jesus says there are only two things required of Christians: to love God and to love one another as we love ourselves (Mark 12.28–34). In this time we love others through our eyes and ears. We listen without interrupting or commenting. We leave silence after each speaker to honour what has been said. The hope is that in the midst of silence and careful listening the speaker is able to hear herself, and thus is able to speak from a deeper place. At times you may want to change the check-in question, such as 'How is your faith being nurtured in this ministry?' or 'How is your family life?'

   This time is valuable because it allows people to 'drop' whatever baggage or turbulence they may be carrying within themselves (joys or anxieties). In this way the sharing helps create more space within them to pray and focus on the work of the group. Youth ministry teams who hold this meeting right before they gather with young people have found that this sharing allows them to clear out (or touch into) anger, frustration or other distractions that might otherwise come out unconsciously among the young people.

Receiving

After listening to one another, we turn our attention more fully to God. This is a time of prayerful listening – full attentiveness to the Spirit of God within and among us. The prayer makes room for these three movements:

1   *Centring:* Our attention shifts from the particularities of the agenda to the One who calls us to this work. We remember who we are and *Whose* we are.
2   *Transformation:* In the silence we become available to God. A new word is given, wounds are tended and renewal takes place.
3   *Call:* We get in touch with the Spirit's longing within us, our calling and the unique way in which God has invited us to live and serve.

Either of the two forms of prayer described in the previous chapter can be used in this time of receiving. I have found it most effective to alternate the group's use of *lectio divina* and the awareness examen.

When the group uses *lectio divina,* a short passage of Scripture is selected to be prayed with. The passage can be chosen from the lectionary, the curriculum being used with the youth group, or selected specifically for the meeting. One person should explain the process of *lectio divina* to the group – *being sure to tell the group how long the silence will last.* After a brief time of silent prayer, the leader slowly reads the passage aloud twice, urging each individual to listen for a word or phrase that jumps out. The group then keeps five to ten minutes of silence, before the leader invites everyone to draw their attention back to the group. [For more on *lectio divina,* see Chapter 5 or Thelma Hall, *Too Deep for Words* (Paulist Press, 1988).]

On alternate meetings the group replaces the *lectio* prayer with the awareness examen. Again, the leader should begin by explaining the prayer to the group and how long the silences will last. The group is then invited to a time of silence. The leader says, 'Ask God to go with you over our last gathering with young people [or whatever other activity is the primary focus of the group] and consider the following question: "For what moment am I most grateful?"' After another few minutes of silence and contemplation, the leader then says, 'As you're ready, ask God to go back with you over our last gathering with young people and consider, "For what moment am I least grateful?"' Allow a few more minutes of silence, before inviting those gathered to draw their attention back to the group. [For more on the awareness examen, see Chapter 8 or Dennis Linn, Sheila Fabricant Linn and Matthew Linn, *Sleeping with Bread* (Paulist Press, 1995).]

Ruminating
In this movement the group takes time to listen to what each person noticed during the prayer time. If the group has prayed *lectio divina*, the leader might say something like, 'I'd like to invite you to share the word that came to you in the prayer and any other noticings or insights that came to you.' If the group does the awareness examen, the leader might say something like, 'I'd like to invite each of us to share what came to us in the prayer, one moment where we were grateful and one moment where we were least grateful.' Allow each person to speak without interruption or commenting. This should be a time of deep listening to how God is speaking to the group.

Reflecting
We then take time to reflect on our call. In this movement we are moving out from our individual sharing to focus on our group identity and group purpose. Someone asks the following question to the group: 'Given all that we've heard and shared, what is God's call to us?' (Some groups replace 'call' with 'invitation'.) The group has an open conversation, allowing silence after each speaker. This is a moment for the group to remember its call and reflect on new words or insights that have come out of the prayer. This should take anything from five to ten minutes.

Responding
The group then begins to address the business items on the agenda. As the group moves into the business, it is important that the leader reminds the group to continue to be aware of the prayer and sharing that has occurred.

Returning
At the end of the meeting the group shares a closing prayer, returning their attention to the Spirit of God. Prayers of gratitude, intercession and blessing may be offered.

*   *   *

It is important to realize from the start that this meeting format may not be as productive as other models for doing business (especially in an immediate sense). Secular business models discard relationships for efficiency; this model does just the opposite. At times people may get frustrated at the amount of time 'wasted' on prayer, checking in and silence. It may feel like 'nothing is getting done'. But the liturgy trusts that waiting on God isn't 'doing nothing'. Something is happening – it's just not under our control. The success of this approach is not measured in productivity, it's better measured by 'fruits' of the Holy Spirit – kindness, generosity, joy, patience, etc. (Galatians 5.22–26). This doesn't mean we don't seek to be productive and mindful of people's time, it just means our first priority is prayer and relationship.

One way to make these meetings even more effective is to share the leadership among the youth ministry volunteers. Take turns leading the prayer or check-in. Find ways to make sure everyone participates in guiding the meeting. The meeting takes on a more communal atmosphere when different people are assigned the different parts of the liturgy. Some groups create a roster so people know weeks ahead of time when they will be responsible for the 'Relating' question or the 'Receiving' prayer.

Many youth ministry groups have found that this meeting is most effective right before or right after a youth meeting/event. It helps the group prepare themselves to minister with the young people and stay close to how the Spirit is asking the leaders to serve.[20]

Testimonies

For eight years I've watched youth ministries and congregations involved with the Youth Ministry and Spirituality Project become transformed as they engage in the liturgy for discernment. I've seen ministries that felt dead and isolated within a congregation come to life – not only with the Spirit of God, but with deepened relationships between adults and youth. As churches begin to create ministries grounded in prayer and relationship, it's not unusual for them to undergo fundamental transformations like the one described here by Chris Berthelsen, a Lutheran pastor and parent of two from St Paul, Minnesota:

> Before we began to practise the liturgy for discernment, we had a youth room with a pool table right in the middle of it. The room looked like a recreation room. As we began to pray and share together and discuss the question, 'What is God's call for us?' we began to sense that we needed to create a youth space that was more sacred and less focused on entertainment or recreation. We shared this with the kids and asked them to pray about it. We were totally surprised when they said they sensed the same thing. So together we dismantled the pool table and had a month of meetings in which we talked about sacred space. We did Bible studies on Moses and the Holy Land and other kinds of lessons that referred to sacred space. Eventually, one of the kids designed a big butterfly that we all painted on one of the walls. We repainted the room as part of a prayer service. When we finished, we all just sat in the room – adults and youth – in awe at what God had led us to do. Now when kids bring their friends to the youth room, they point out the verses and images on the walls. They tell them how the room used to be just a recreation room. They tell the other kids like they're telling them something sacred has happened. And something sacred *has* happened . . .

Another of my favourite stories about the power of gathering people together to pray and discern on behalf of young people occurred in a small Episcopal church in a central Colorado ski town. The congregation was ageing and at first resisted their new priest's attempts to create a youth ministry. As one elder told me, 'We are a dying congregation. We need a hospice ministry, not a youth ministry.' The young priest asked the church vestry if he could spend a portion of his hours seeking to discover whether God was calling the congregation to form a ministry with young people. He agreed to abandon his efforts if the church were unable to establish a youth ministry within two years. The vestry reluctantly agreed, but warned him that he would be unable to find adults within the congregation to support such a ministry, much less to serve in it.

Father James and his wife, Eli, came out to a training programme in which I taught the calling process and liturgy for discernment. They went back to their parish and slowly began to pray, discern and share the vision of a youth ministry with other church members. Within a month they were pleasantly surprised to find eight adults – mostly elderly – within their 200-member congregation who sensed a call to youth ministry. After a day-long retreat the group began to meet weekly, faithfully following the liturgy for discernment. Together they would pray, share their lives and discern what actions they could undertake in order to welcome the town's young people into the church.

One year later I contacted James to ask how it was going. 'Well,' he told me, 'we haven't attracted any youth to the church yet.' But he told me that after a year of prayer and sharing, the ministry team had noticed 'home' was becoming a recurring theme and image. He told me they had really begun to care for one another and often met for dinner outside of their meetings. He told me two of the members had undergone severe family crisis and that the group had worked hard to care for one another. He ended, however, by telling me he was disappointed they still did not have a youth ministry. He was beginning to sense that he should direct his energy in other directions.

Two months later I was in Colorado and showed up at James' church a few minutes before worship. James spotted me and rushed over. 'You're not going to believe what happened last night,' he told me, bursting with excitement. 'You'll have to hear it in worship.' I went inside the sanctuary and sat down. After the prelude, James came to the front and told the congregation 'something tremendous' had occurred that he needed to share.

One month earlier a young man had died of alcohol poisoning after a night of partying and drinking with his buddies. James had read about the tragedy in the paper. A few days later he was in a coffee shop when two guys in their early twenties noticed James wearing his white collar, came up to him, and asked if he were a priest. They then asked, 'Do you do memorial services?' He told them he did, and invited them to sit down. James listened as they told him it was their friend who had died. Then they began to talk about their lives in Colorado. They told James that they and many of their friends came from broken homes, and many of them went from ski town to ski town looking for work and parties. They talked about sleeping in cars and working odd jobs within this upscale resort town. James continued to listen. They told him their friend was from New York, and that his parents had flown his body back home for the funeral. None of them had the money to go back east for the service. They asked James if he could hold some sort of memorial service in town so they could mourn the death of their friend. James agreed to do it and a date was set.

The next week James met with the youth ministry team. While they were sharing he told them about the upcoming memorial service. He asked for volunteers to help prepare and serve food for the young people. Everyone agreed to help out. James said he expected a small gathering of five to ten people. On the day of the service the youth ministry team showed up early. They transformed the fellowship room of the church. They wanted it to feel like you were visiting your favourite grandmother's house. They placed homemade tablecloths, little bouquets of flowers and bowls of candy on each of the tables. They had three kinds of soup simmering in the kitchen and fresh-baked cookies placed on platters around the room. They made sandwiches, cut them in triangles and placed them on each table, ready for the group's arrival.

When it came time for the service, James said, 'It was like the underbelly of our town showed up.' Over 100 young adults, ages 16 to 25, gathered in the sanctuary, dressed in baggy pants, knit hats, worn military fatigues and other rough snow-gear. James ran back to the fellowship hall and told the youth ministry team to prepare more food. The group hurried to the grocery store and soon formed a sandwich assembly line while 68-year-old Glenda made another pot of corn chowder.

At the close of the service, James invited the young people to stay for food. Every one of them stayed. For the next five hours the young 'ski bums' ate soup and sandwiches and poured their hearts out to the listening adults. One woman later told me, 'Most of us have lived long enough to have friends and even close family die . . . so we knew how to listen and be with these kids who were in grief.'

The adults noticed that many of the young people had holes in their shoes and clothes. They went over to the long-neglected 'donation' box placed in the narthex of the church. They found clean pants, shoes and warm jackets. They brought them to the fellowship hall and offered them to the young people. They were ecstatic! When the evening finally started to wind down, one of the young men asked if they could come to the church again sometime.

That night, after clean-up, the youth ministry team gathered. They talked about the great need among these discarded youth within their town for food, friendship and clothing. They talked about how much they had enjoyed talking and being with these young adults who often appeared rough and distant. They prayed. They listened to how God was calling them to serve. An idea emerged. Each month they would have a night like this – a night where they served good food, handed out clothing and spent time just hanging out with these young adults.

As James stood in the front of the church that Sunday and told this story, he became emotional and said, 'We have a ministry, people. We have a ministry. We need every one of you to buy groceries and bring them to the church. We need each of you to go through your closets and bring any shoes, pants and warm clothes you can spare. We need people to show up on the first Saturday night each month to serve and listen to these young people. We need everyone to participate. God is not finished with this church yet. We have a ministry to do. We have young people to welcome.'

A few months later James sent me a copy of a flyer that he and the youth ministry team had posted in motel break rooms, lift-operator stations and fast-food restaurants where young people gathered. The poster had a picture of a warm, friendly grandmother working over a hot stove and read, 'Grandma's Home Cooking. Fresh-made soup. Home-baked cookies. Free shoes, jackets and pants. A listening ear. Everyone's welcome. First Saturday of each month. St John's Episcopal Church.' Sixty young people showed up the next month and the month after that. Some of these young people began to inquire about the symbols in the sanctuary. Others asked if they could come to worship.

What's remarkable about this story is that James and the youth ministry team followed God's timing. They had the trust and patience to spend a *year* meeting for prayer, sharing and deep listening before discerning God's leading. When they finally began a youth ministry, it looked very different from anything they had expected, and was a much more natural fit with their gifts than if they tried to emulate the ministries of other churches.

The liturgy for discernment is just one way in which God's presence and guidance can be made central to our ministries. There are many other ways in which a youth ministry might become more transparent to God's leading and calling. Whatever the method, my experience has been that as churches gather on behalf of young people in prayer, relationship and trust, a ministry begins to emerge that is organic and life-giving to both youth and adults. Over time relationships begin to develop, and the cultural divide between youth and adults begins to dissipate. Suddenly, it becomes unclear who is giving and who is receiving. Suddenly, the youth ministry becomes a setting in which both youth and adults are growing together in their life with God.

11

Noticing

———◈———

I think the most powerful aspect of contemplative youth ministry has been giving young people the space and opportunity to notice God in their lives. Creating exercises where kids can notice God invites a sense of wonder. Simply asking, 'What did you notice?' has caused senior high students, junior high students, Sunday school teachers, congregational members and myself to 'see God' in our ordinary days. As I've asked kids to tell me where they encounter God in worship, I've heard all kinds of wonderful responses: 'When I lit the candles.' 'In the stained-glass windows.' 'In my father's eyes during the sermon.' 'In the sharing of the peace.' 'In the sound of my own voice saying the Lord's Prayer.'

(Chris Berthelsen, pastor, First Lutheran Church, St Paul, Minnesota)

I mean, teens nowadays are so busy and so stressed out, that it's kind of hard to imagine them ever sitting still contemplating and noticing God in their lives, but it really does work. It just came naturally and more naturally than I'd ever, you know, thought. And I've taken it home. My mom knows that if I'm up at six in the morning and there's a little sticky note on my door that she shouldn't come in, it's because I'm usually sitting there sitting in silence praying. And I know my parents notice a difference in the way I act toward others. After I've had that time to just be silent and I guess be held by God, there's a difference, you know – how I talk to others, my reaction time, what I get offended by is completely changed when I've already taken that time to be within myself and then respond to other people.

There's a quote I heard from one of the spiritual directors at a youth event. It's from St Seraphim. He said, 'If you alone find God, thousands around you will be saved.' And that's very true in contemplative prayer. I really believe it's about the way you treat others after you come inside yourself and see what's important and what's in your heart and how God's speaking to you. There's a complete difference.

(Lauren, age 16, Cleveland, Ohio)

Most of this book has focused on the disposition and practice of adults in youth ministry. This is important because adults hold the power and set the climate for spiritual formation. As Gina Yeager, Director of Youth Ministry for the Presbyterian Church USA, once said to me, 'Youth ministry is just as much about adults as it is youth.' Yet the questions remain: What do we do with the kids? How does a contemplative attitude affect our ministry with youth?

Young people need adults who have gained wisdom through their personal experience of God. But our desire for young people isn't just that they'll be surrounded by adults who know God. It's deeper than that. It's that young people will begin to recognize and experience God's presence for themselves. This is the hope: that more and more young people will begin to see, hear, know and nurture God's presence within the intimacies of their lives and their interactions with the larger world.

Our first task as youth ministers is to seek to be with young people just as Jesus was with people. Our second task is to help them develop the eyes, ears and heart of Jesus for themselves. We are not only called to be witnesses among young people, we are also called, like Jesus, to be teachers. We are called to awaken young people to the presence of God in the world.

Much of my understanding and practice of youth formation comes from my experience in spiritual direction. Spiritual directors are people who have the gift of spiritual friendship. Just as in contemplation, a good spiritual director is someone who seeks to be present and attentive. They are a second pair of ears and eyes who listen and look for signs of God within the experience of others. Spiritual directors aren't experts on God; just the opposite, a good spiritual director is very aware of their ignorance, blindness and limitations in regard to the spiritual lives of others. They trust that God is doing the ministry, so they are satisfied to stand on the sidelines of a person's life and simply reflect what they are seeing.

Author and Episcopal priest Alan Jones tells the story of the first person who came to him for spiritual direction. Alan was young – just out of seminary and still unsure of his vocation. An elderly monk who was a renowned scholar and a deep man of prayer, considered a saint by his community, came to Alan and said, 'Alan, I want you to be my spiritual director.'

'But brother, I can't!' Alan pleaded.

With a twinkle in his eye, the wise monk responded: 'I know!' [21]

The older teacher knew that the real director was the Holy Spirit, not Alan, and that Alan would do fine as a spiritual director as long as he didn't rely on his own skills. As youth ministers we seek the same humility. We trust that God is the real director of young people's souls – our role is to notice, to point, to help when asked, and to avoid relying too heavily on our own skills and learning.

There is a simple and beautiful way in which Elizabeth Liebert, Professor of Spiritual Life at San Francisco Theological Seminary, describes the movements within a spiritual direction relationship. These movements are *noticing, naming* and *nurturing*. Noticing refers to the way in which we help people (through careful attentiveness) become more aware of their experience of God. Naming involves aiding people in finding language and theology for their experience. And finally, nurturing concerns the ways we help people develop practices and disciplines that deepen their relationship with God.

In the next three chapters, I want to explore this triptych to reveal how we might help young people respond to Jesus' invitation to freedom. This chapter will focus on 'noticing' – helping youth become aware of their experience of God. The two chapters that follow will explore 'naming' (helping youth find words for the experience of God) and 'nurturing' (helping young people develop practices that deepen their understanding and relationship with God).

Noticing

The human heart, be it young or old, longs to experience the presence of God. Religious words and symbols, no matter how inspiring, are not enough. We all desire to know God for ourselves. 'Don't just tell me about Jesus', young people seem to say. 'Let me meet Jesus for myself.'

As we seek to become contemplative ministers, we not only strive to deepen our own awareness of God within our ministries, we also seek to help *young people* open their eyes and ears to the movement of God. One way we do this is by noticing. Knowing that God is present and at work within each and every young person, we attend to them like watchmen waiting for the morning. We wait patiently, seeking to become aware of the ways in which Jesus is courting our youth. We invite young people to see for themselves. We encourage them to look for God, to listen for God, to reach out and seek God with all their heart, mind, soul and strength. We tell them, 'Don't take my word for it. Go ahead. Taste and see that the Lord is good.'

In order to help young people notice God, we must trust that all teenagers know something of God. If we trust that God is present with us in the world, then we know that all young people have some experience of God. These experiences are like seeds that need to be seen, nurtured and tended until they bloom. Our first task as youth ministers is simply to help young people notice their experiences of God. Unfortunately, most young people have gone through some sort of spiritual 'deformation'. They have been taught that God exists only in the Bible, in ancient times, or in other, holier people. Conventional, word-heavy, Christian education programmes give the impression that God is distant, abstract, a reality only for ministers and the religiously trained. More charismatic youth ministries can give the equally false assumption that God is present only in the spectacular – miraculous healings, powerful speakers, mystical saints and life-changing testimonies.

Unfortunately, what's rarely communicated to young people is that the experience of God is actually quite ordinary and even common: Jesus claims to be present whenever two or three are gathered in his name; 'God is love', we're told in 1 John – intimating that God is present in every true experience of love; Paul writes that moments of joy, patience and kindness are experiences of the Holy Spirit. Figures in the New Testament encountered Jesus while working, eating, praying, conversing, travelling and engaging in other ordinary human experiences. As youth ministers we don't need to convince young people of the presence of God. We don't need to 'deliver' God to young people. We simply need to help young people notice the ways in which each and every one of them is already in relationship with God. Our role is to help young people notice the ways in which Jesus is already near, already seeking trust and friendship.

How do we help young people notice their experience of God?

1. We point

More ministers need to take their cues from John the Baptist. Not only were John's eyes and ears open to the presence of God, he also sought to help others notice God. John was a pointer. When John sees Jesus coming to be baptized, he singles him out to his followers and says, 'Here is the Lamb of God . . .' (John 1.29). One of the first ways we can help young people become more aware of their life in God is to point to the moments when Jesus seems near. We notice when young people are alive, when their hearts are 'burning' within them (see Luke 24.32). We notice when they seem open to God. We notice when young people are living like Jesus. We notice when the fruits of the Spirit are present in them – when they're giving or receiving love, joy, peace, patience, kindness, generosity, faithfulness and gentleness. We hold up these moments to young people until they notice it for themselves – until they see that they are in the stream of God's love, that they are participating in Jesus' way of life.

For seven years I took youth groups from Oregon and California on week-long house-building projects among the shanty towns that exist just across the US border in Mexico. These trips were transformative for both youth and adults, as we sought to live in community with Mexican citizens, many of whom were struggling to find work in the border factories that provide cheap goods for US consumers.

On one particular trip I spent a few days working with a group of teens from a US suburb who were deeply motivated to build a home for a Mexican family that included a mother, father, grandmother and four small children. The group arrived early at the worksite eager to get started. The appreciative mother and grandmother sat on fruit crates smiling and grateful at the prospect of a new home while the children ran around the worksite enamoured by the teenagers with their tool belts and baseball caps. During our first lunch break, the children were eager to interact with our group. They stood by, wide-eyed, as we took out sack lunches filled with stuffed deli sandwiches, juice drinks, fruit and cookies. One teenage girl, Clare, noticed the disparity between her lunch and the few lime-sprinkled tortillas the children were sharing. She gestured discreetly for the children to come and sit by her. I watched as she carefully divided her lunch, giving equal parts to each of the four children, who received the gifts with grateful smiles and ate giggling with glee.

As the teens went back to work I noticed that the oldest of the four, a boy about nine years of age, took off running to a field at the edge of the makeshift community. A few minutes later he returned, holding a small bouquet of yellow flowers. He stood patiently at the edge of the worksite, watching as Clare crouched on her hands and knees spreading cement. I went back to work, but from time to time noticed the boy, sometimes standing, sometimes sitting, holding his small cluster of flowers, waiting to catch Clare's attention. We finished the foundation and soon were deep in mud and water rinsing and cleaning our tools. Clare finished up and jumped into the back of our work truck. I watched as the boy followed her and stood by the back of the truck, now holding a tired and wilting bunch of flowers. He called over the side of the truck, 'Senorita. Senorita.' Clare was busy chatting with her friends and comparing scratches and bruises from a hard day of work, and was unaware of the boy. One of our adult leaders jumped in the cab of the truck and soon Clare, her friends and the bed of tools were bouncing back to our campsite.

The next day a different youth group requested additional workers at another site that was proving particularly difficult. Clare volunteered to leave her own youth group and help. For the next three days she built walls, nailed roofing and spread stucco with the help of teenagers from a different town than her own. Finally, on the last day of our trip, Clare returned to her friends and the original worksite with the four children. Clare was excited to see her friends and immediately became immersed in conversation. She talked and worked with her two best buddies so intensely that she hardly noticed the nine-year-old boy following her throughout her activities. I noticed, however, that from time to time the boy would call to her saying, 'Senorita. Senorita.' A few times Clare heard the boy and smiled or patted his head, but continued to work and talk with her friends. As the day came to a close, so did our work on the house. The roof and walls were complete, prompting the group to give a great cheer. The family was brought together in front of the simple dwelling and presented with gifts – blankets, food and toys for the kids. I noticed again as the oldest boy moved closer to Clare, tugging on her shirt. She turned and gave him a quick and somewhat perfunctory hug, then returned to chatting excitedly with her friends while the boy stood, once again, waiting for her attention.

After a prayer and many hugs, we all ran for the vans, hoping to beat the descending darkness. I counted the kids to make sure no one was left behind, grabbed a seat, shut the door, and then took one last look at the worksite. I spied a sweatshirt that someone had left behind. I asked the driver to wait as I stepped out of the car and ran to get the shirt. As I returned to the vehicle I noticed the same boy who'd spent the day seeking Clare's attention. He was standing at the rear of the van, crying and looking up through the back window where Clare was seated. Remembering how persistently he'd sought Clare's attention, I went to the van, told the driver to turn off the engine, and asked Clare to step out and go and see the boy. She was startled at first, but agreed and soon made her way through her friends, climbed out of the van, walked over to the boy and for the first time since their lunch together, knelt down and gave him her full attention.

The boy smiled at her with wet eyes, then reached into his back pocket, took out a small handful of crushed yellow flowers and offered them to her. Clare looked at the crumpled offering quizzically at first, but then realized what was taking place. 'Para la comida' ['For the food'], he said. Clare carefully brushed the flowers from his hand into hers, wrapped her fingers around the tender gift, closed her eyes, and held it to her heart. The boy smiled with relief. Then he wrapped his arms around her neck and pressed his cheek against hers and hung there for a long minute. He stepped away, walked back to his family, turned and waved.

There have been a few precious moments in my life as a minister when I've had the privilege to witness a young person's heart break open to the mystery of God's love. This was one of them. I watched as Clare looked at that boy. I watched as she looked down at the frail gift in her hands. I watched as she climbed back into the van, holding the present she'd received, and then gazed back through the window at the boy and his family. And I knew, just as she knew, that she would no longer be the same.

By pointing out the crying boy to Clare, I was able to point to the way in which the Holy Spirit was present. Pulling Clare from the energy of her friends, I helped her notice the way God's grace was pursuing her. Had I not stopped the van driver and asked Clare to be with the boy, she might have never received the gift of the boy's gratitude, she might have forgotten her own act of generosity and kindness, she might have missed the way she was participating in God's work of love. Just as Jesus tells people again and again, 'Your faith has made you well', we seek to point out the moments when teenagers are living in faith, sometimes even before they have claimed it for themselves. We pay attention to the moments when their hearts are open and then we point and say, 'You seem to really care about those people.' We say, 'You seem more yourself – why is that?' We reflect, 'You're so alive today.' We then offer, 'Here is the Lamb of God.' 'This is the Christian life.' 'This is the experience of God the Bible speaks of. God is here. The kingdom of God is within you. You're living like Jesus. Can you see it?'

2. We question

Another way we help young people notice God is by simply asking them, 'How is God present?' I ask this question when they are at play, when they are with their friends, when they reflect on their home situations or future vocations. Like a good spiritual director I want to continually invite young people to reflect on God's presence within their experiences: 'How is God present? Where do you notice God? How is Jesus among us?'

When I ask young people to turn their attention to the presence of God, a number of things take place. First, I'm reminding them that God is present and available. This is especially powerful if I ask this question while they talk about a school situation, a moment of pain or suffering, or a seemingly mundane experience. When I ask them to notice God, I'm communicating the possibility that each and every moment of our lives is alive with the presence of God. Second, the question also communicates that young people have the capacity to notice God. There is a sense of empowerment as I invite them to be 'religious interpreters' – people who can perceive and become aware of the movement of God. Third, I'm helping them reflect on their real-life theologies and religious biases. When I ask a young person, 'How is God present in this moment?' she may respond, 'I don't think God has anything to do with my school – God is just about praying and church.' To ask young people to notice God is to invite them to reflect on their beliefs concerning God's relationship to the world. Finally, when I ask a young person to notice the Holy in their midst, I'm helping them develop their sensitivity to God. They have to pause, become aware of what they're seeing, hearing, feeling and thinking.

By asking young people how God is present, we invite them to reflect as full conversation partners within the Christian faith. The Bible was written by people who asked themselves how God was present in their experiences and then wrote down what they noticed. When young people are allowed to reflect on this question, they are given respect as full conversation partners.

When I was working as a youth minister in Portland, Oregon, there was a group of girls who would cut class in the middle of the day and gather on a downtown corner to smoke cigarettes. Over time I befriended them and one day they asked about my job as a minister. I responded with something like, 'I'm trying to help people become increasingly aware of God's presence in their lives and in the world.'

'Well, I can tell you God isn't in my life,' said one young woman, whom I later learned had been abused and abandoned by her father. We talked for a while, then I asked if they would try an experiment with me. I asked them to move back from the kerb and stand against the outside wall of a coffee shop, observing the sights around them. I invited them to look at the cars and the people, the trees across the street, the buildings and the cloud formations in the sky. 'Just for a moment, allow yourself to believe in God,' I said. 'Just suspend your doubt for a moment and imagine that God is present in the world . . . Then reflect on how God would be here, in this moment.' For about five minutes the girls stood taking in the activity around them. I asked them what they noticed.

'God would be in that sleeping drunk across the street, waiting for someone to give him a place to sleep.'

'I think God would be in the sound of the birds singing in those trees. I don't know if anyone notices, but I do every time I'm down here – and it makes me peaceful.'

On and on they went, noticing the God they didn't believe in. And then the girl who'd been abandoned by her father said, 'If God exists, he would be in the seeds of the grass that are still waiting for the sunlight, waiting to grow, underneath the pavement and cement.'

For the next six months I met with this group of young women. Each week we'd talk, drink coffee, and then I'd ask the question, 'Where is God in this moment?' Together we'd respond and reflect. They'd listen to me. I would listen to them. Eventually, a few of them began attending our church youth group and became followers of Jesus. But the girl who had been abandoned slowly disappeared into the streets. A number of years later, I ran into one of the street-corner smokers. I asked about her friend who had been abandoned by her father. She told me she'd become addicted to heroin, then contracted AIDS and disappeared from the area. I was shocked. I felt deeply saddened by the news and grieved not doing more to reach out to her. She was right, I thought, God was in the grass seeds – her own fading hope, underneath the black pavement, waiting for the sun.

3. We invite

Another powerful way in which young people notice their relationship with God is through prayer – listening forms of prayer that make space for young people to encounter God directly. Every time I lead a Sunday school class or youth group meeting, I try to create a setting where young people can explore their experience and relationship with God. Traditional forms of youth ministry are often word-heavy, placing the teacher as the sole mediator of God. The teacher talks about God, the teacher leads the discussion about God, and then the teacher closes in prayer. In this model, a young person's relationship with the holy is only through the teacher. As long as the teacher is approachable and trustworthy, the young people are willing to listen; however, there comes a point when the words of faith become empty if young people aren't given the opportunity to experience the God behind the teaching.

There are many ways in which we can invite young people to turn and notice God directly within their experience. Often these are called 'spiritual exercises' – exercises that encourage youth to intentionally explore their relationship with God. There are many books containing prayer exercises that can be used with young people.[22] Here are a few of the exercises I've found particularly helpful.

Creative prayer

Clay, crayons, paints and paper – all of these materials can help facilitate a young person's awareness of God. They are especially helpful for younger teens, who can find silent prayer abstract and uncomfortable. Sometimes I use these materials with very open instructions. I ask young people to take some paper and a handful of crayons. I invite them to find a space where they can pray. I invite them to turn to God in prayer and say something like, 'God, how are you present in my life at this time?' I instruct them to wait in silence until they feel ready to express what they notice through the colours and paper. I remind them this isn't an art exercise – there's no grade, no expectation as to how their image might unfold. I tell them they might only find one colour that expresses their experience of God and spend the time scribbling with that particular colour, or they might have a particular image that seems important and spend the prayer time exploring that image. I give the youth 15 or 20 minutes to pray with the colours (or clay or other creative medium), then I ask them to come together and share what they noticed. 'How was God with you in this prayer? What did you notice about your relationship with God in this exercise?'

Sometimes I offer more direct instructions. I say, 'Pray with the colours, asking Jesus to show you the ways in which he is grateful for you.' Or, 'As you pray with the clay, ask how God is present within the problems or suffering you face in your life.' I've found exercises with art media to be particularly powerful when led with a sense of both prayer and playfulness.

Walking prayer
Prayers that give them permission to use their bodies are often easier for youth to engage. One of the spiritual exercises I've found most helpful with young people is to invite them to take a walk with Jesus. After a few moments of silence I invite them to go outside and then, in their own way, ask Jesus to walk with them. I ask them to refrain from talking or walking with others, but instead, to take their time strolling around the neighbourhood, noticing the sights and sounds that catch their attention. I tell them to spend extra time with anything that seems to stand out and grab their interest.

Sometimes, when working with kids who are still very sceptical, I'll say something like, 'As you go on your walk, say the following prayer: "God, if you exist, help me to notice you during this time."' I give kids about 15 minutes to walk, then have them gather back together in silence. After everyone has returned, I ask them to share their experiences.

I remember working with a youth group that had two 'skater' boys who were forced to attend church and resisted all forms of spiritual reflection. I invited them to take a prayer walk as an experiment – seeking to see if they noticed God's presence while they meandered through the surrounding neighbourhood. Surprisingly, they did the exercise. When they returned, I asked them what they noticed. One of the skater boys raised his hand and shared, 'I immediately walked to the street where I like to skate-board. I walked slowly and prayed just as you told us to. For some reason, as I was walking I felt like I should look up. When I did, I noticed these incredible tree branches reaching out from both sides of the street, covering the street like a canopy. The leaves were red and orange, filtering the sun. I lay down on my back on the sidewalk and just looked at these trees. I couldn't believe I'd never noticed them before. It was like they were these big arms, covering the street, protecting the place where I skate. I was so amazed. I just kept saying, 'Is this you, God? Is this you?'

Walking prayers can be used after Bible studies or lesson times to give young people a chance to reflect on the material with God. For example, after a lesson on service, young people can be invited to take a prayer walk, asking God to help them reflect on how he is drawing them to serve. Or after studying the prodigal son, or the grateful leper, youth can be asked to take a prayerful walk asking God to reflect with them on their experience of gratitude or repentance.

The awareness examen
Ignatius' examination of conscience (see Chapter 8) is a simple way to help young people notice their experience of God. I've used the examen at the beginning of Sunday school classes, in youth meetings, mission trips, meal times, and even informal get-togethers with youth. The examen gives young people the op-portunity to catch their breath, savour their experience and notice the ways God is present in their lives. I invite youth to look over their day and ask God to bring to them all the moments of grace (or sometimes I replace 'grace' with 'gratitude' or 'love').[23] I invite them to choose one of these moments to reflect on in the silence: 'How is God present in this experience? What is God's invitation to you in this experience?' I give them a few moments to rest in gratitude for whatever moment has come to their attention. Then I invite them to share their experiences with the group.

One time the youth in my church decided to practise the examen each night during the 40 days of Lent. Adults from the church paired up with each young person, and the pair spoke every night and practised the prayer over the phone. After Easter we held an all-church retreat where some of the youth and adults shared their experiences. Of particular interest to me was that each person, young and old, found that they began to experience great transformation through this simple exercise. As they practised the examen, they became more mindful of God's presence during their days. They found themselves seeking to live more fully into the places and experiences where they'd noticed God's grace, and sought to move through the moments where they'd noticed resistance to God's love. The effect was that they found their daily lives more imbued with a sense of God's love and presence.

Silent prayer
When I meet with youth in a youth group or Sunday school setting, I often engage the young people in Bible study on a particular subject, story or parable. After we've spent some time discussing a particular Scripture, I then invite the youth to turn their attention to God. I ask them to allow themselves to be with God directly in the midst of whatever content we've explored. If we're reading the Psalms and discussing suffering, I light a candle at the close of the discussion and ask the youth to close their eyes and simply rest with God beneath all we've discussed. We allow the words to settle down. I then invite them to pray in the silence, 'God, how have you been present in this discussion? What do you seek to teach us?' After a few minutes of silence I invite kids to share. In this way, we make space for God – space for young people to engage God directly in the midst of our conversation and learning. In the Quaker tradition, people sometimes call for silence in the midst of a meeting. The call for silence is an invitation to stop, turn to God and listen. I try to call for silence in the midst of work projects, lessons, play time and conversation. The call to stop and listen – even if it's just for 30 seconds, is another opportunity for young people to turn and notice God within their experiences.

I try to incorporate silence into every youth event and youth meeting. Over time, I have found that these times of quiet become more and more attractive to young people. Recently, while leading a week-long youth camp, I invited kids to spend a whole afternoon in silent prayer. After a few words about the silent prayer tradition, I sent them out along a deserted coastline to pray and be with God in silent communion. At the end of our event, I asked kids to rate their most significant experiences of the week. I was shocked to find that the majority of kids listed the silent time on the coast as their favourite experience – even when compared to day trips to San Francisco, recreational games and free time with friends.

Contemplative prayer

Classical forms of contemplative prayer such as *lectio divina,* Ignatian contemplation and even centring prayer can be incredibly fruitful for young people in helping them deepen their awareness of God. A friend who serves in a United Methodist church practises *lectio divina* with the young people in her confirmation programme. She's found that at the end of the year, kids continually cite *lectio divina* as the most significant part of the class.

It's reasonable to offer some modifications when leading these prayers with youth. Remember that youth, like adults, live in a multi-tasking, attention-demanding culture that presents them with a barrage of sights, sounds and temptations. Silence and prayer can be incredibly difficult. Make sure you are informal when inviting youth into silence. Add some humour. The more you try to make the prayer pristine and 'spiritual', the more the kids are going to feel uncomfortable and start giggling. Acknowledge that it might feel awkward. Use an experimental tone. Say things like, 'I know this may seem strange; let's try this as an experiment. We're going to take three minutes of silence to just spend time resting in God. You may find your mind wandering. You may feel like fidgeting. All of that's okay – we're only seeing what it's like to just rest and be with God.'

Make sure you use very short periods of silence when first exposing kids to contemplative prayer – even 30 seconds can seem like a long time. I once led a junior high group where we spent a month only taking 10 to 15 seconds of silence. After a year the kids could handle about 30 seconds. A year later we spent almost five minutes in silence each time we met. It takes time to get used to just being with God.

The environment can be a help or hindrance when leading kids in contemplative prayer. Set a mood that's conducive to silence.

Turn out the lights and light a candle. Go outside under the stars. Play some music that helps youth settle down. Make sure there's plenty of space. Or better yet, ask the youth to set the room up for contemplative prayer. I find youth very receptive to contemplative prayer, especially when led by adults who are experienced in prayer and can lead it with a sense of 'lightness'.

A note of caution: it can be incredibly painful and even destructive for kids to be led into contemplative prayer or a spiritual exercise by people who have little experience. I've had too many painful experiences of watching adults who had little experience in contemplative prayer try to lead kids in such exercises. Often, they create high expectations, creating a heavy atmosphere where kids feel expected to produce an experience of God. In Appendix 4 at the end of this book, you'll find a guideline for leading a prayer exercise with youth. I urge you to use this guideline – it has been refined over the years by many youth workers as they have sought to help kids pray contemplatively.

Of course, the best way to learn how to lead kids in prayer is to spend time in prayer. Go on prayer retreats, read books on prayer, and most importantly spend time in prayer yourself. As you cultivate your own life of prayer, you'll learn more about how to help kids pray and how to respond when they face difficulties in their own prayer lives.

4. We create circumstances
'It is circumstances, not ideas, that change people', author and Catholic priest Richard Rohr once said.[24] Possibly the most significant way we can help young people notice their experience of God is by helping them engage real life. It's amazing how much time young people spend in 'virtual life'. I'm not just talking about the time spent in front of televisions, computers and video devices (statistics say most teens spend more than 24 hours a week!). I'm also referring to school, where most youth spend the majority of their daylight hours. Young people often feel the message they receive in school, in church and in their own families is that life begins after college. It begins once they're married and have a good job. There's a sense that the time spent in school and church isn't 'real life', just preparation for real life. It's a great

disservice to young people if our youth ministry programmes communicate this same message.

We can help young people notice the presence of God by helping them to see that their lives have already begun, that their decisions matter, that their lives have meaning and can help bring care and change into the world right now. This is why it's important to get kids out of the youth room or Sunday school class and into the streets. It's important to take kids on trips where they meet new and different kinds of people. It's important to give them situations where they can work and serve and make a difference. Then, in these real-life settings, ask them, 'How is God present here?' I ask youth to notice how they feel – scared, frightened, sad, happy – and then ask them how God might be within these feelings.

I've always felt it was my responsibility to invite young people to have their hearts broken by the things that break Jesus' heart. Just as Jesus enters into the lives of suffering people, so I too have tried to invite young people into the suffering places within humanity. Jesus tells us these places of suffering are places where he is most available. I want young people to listen to people who have suffered tragedy and hardship. I want them to befriend people who spend their days seeking food and clean water. I want them to experience some of the hopelessness that exists in this world, so that they can make contact with the suffering of God, so that they can sense the compassion of Jesus, so they can feel God calling them to be a source of life and healing in this world.

A few years ago I participated in the leadership for a week-long contemplative retreat with high school students. We began each day with a morning prayer service that involved silence and contemplative prayer. Throughout the day we told kids stories of different contemplative saints within the Christian tradition and led them through various prayer exercises. On the fourth day of the week we decided to take the youth out of the chapel and into the streets. We took them to a Franciscan community in the Tenderloin district of San Francisco that provides lunch to over 2,500 homeless people each day. We showed up to help serve in the kitchen. But when one of the brothers in the community met us, he told us it would be much more significant to simply spend some time eating and visiting with people. We dispersed the youth throughout the serpentine line of hungry people. They waited for half an hour or so, shuffling up to the front door of the building toward the kitchen. The youth introduced themselves to the folks in line and spent the lunchtime eating and conversing. For the rest of the afternoon we hung out on the street listening to people's stories, then ended the day in St Basil's Chapel where many of the homeless in that area gather to rest and pray.

On our way back home one young girl from Omaha, Nebraska, told me she would soon graduate from high school and had planned to become a hairdresser. She revealed, however, that after spending time with folks in the city, she had made a commitment to God to become a teacher and serve people like the ones she'd met in the Tenderloin. I thought it was a beautiful dream, but didn't know how much weight to give it. Four years later I received a letter from the youth worker in this young girl's parish. In the letter he told me that the young woman who had spent that day in the Tenderloin district had nearly completed her teaching certificate and was looking for a job in one of the poorer neighbourhoods of Omaha. I've had countless similar experiences in which young people, placed within the centre of human life and struggle, hear God's love and call.

Slow Club

My son Joseph is a natural contemplative. When he was four years old, he was no longer willing to be hustled to pre-school and hurried along on errands. One morning Joseph announced he was starting a new organization called 'Slow Club', in which he would serve as president. The rules of the club were simple: no running and no hurrying. Unfortunately, neither his parents nor his brother could commit to these regulations, so for the next year Joseph was the only member of his club. Each morning, he'd stroll to school at his natural pace. If I tried to pull him along or anxiously urge him to 'Hurry it up!' he'd respond calmly, 'I'm president of Slow Club, Dad. I don't hurry.'

At night over dinner, Joseph would talk about his club. He told us about the things he noticed during the day and shook his head at the other children who always seemed too busy to see the marvels and treasures so clearly visible to the patient eye: a piece of wire, a bottle cap, an especially smooth rock, a line of ants. From time to time he'd invite neighbours or other friends to join his organization, but no one could commit to his charter.

One summer while I was teaching at a youth camp, Joseph granted me a one-day membership to his club. After playing ultimate Frisbee with a group of teenagers, the bell rang for lunch. The kids bolted toward the dining hall. Joseph had been watching the game, so I ran over to him, put on my sweatshirt, grabbed his hand and began pulling him hastily behind the group. I was hungry and wanted to get a place in line. Joseph reminded me, however, that I'd accepted his one-day club membership and would need to reduce my speed drastically. I took a deep breath and reluctantly slowed to my son's pace. Joseph looked at me satisfied, then said, 'You see, Dad, when you slow down, you notice things. Just look around as we walk, and you'll see things everyone else has missed.'

Quietly we strolled through the campground, looking carefully at our surroundings. Suddenly, I saw something move off to the side of the path. 'Joseph!' I whispered excitedly. 'Look over there.' He turned, and we both saw two jackrabbits, standing on their hind legs, watching us. Joseph gave me a knowing smile and said, 'I bet we're the only ones who noticed those rabbits.' We walked on – stopping to look at butterflies, strange purple wild flowers, enormous beetles, and a lizard with half a tail. When we joined the rest of the family, we both talked excitedly about the treasures we'd seen.

Like Joseph, those of us who minister among young people seek to be members of Slow Club. We invite young people to attend to their lives; we encourage them not to overlook the signs of God's presence. Every time we're among young people, we look and listen with slow eyes and ears. We listen for the deep sounds of God. We look patiently for the little signs of grace. We cultivate wonder. Like Joseph, we walk beside them saying, 'What do you notice? What do you see? How is God present in this moment?'

I want to be a member of Slow Club. I want to be a still and knowing presence among young people. I want to walk beside them, stopping from time to time to notice the God who waits to be received.

12

Naming

———◆———

Although I didn't realize it at the time, my interaction with our teens was more about conveying a quick burst of information ('Hi. How are you? Great, now let me tell you what you need to know . . .') and less about actually listening. My relationship with our teens was pretty superficial. As I was introduced to and started to regularly practice contemplative prayer, I found myself slowing down in a variety of ways. With my youth that meant not asking a question until I was ready to really listen to the answer. It also meant not being anxious to move on to the next teen, but instead to be comfortable listening to the teen's responses, however long they took. I also noticed I was much more likely to ask some follow-up questions to get a deeper understanding of what was happening in their lives. My transformation allows me to start from a point of deeper interest and slowly bring them into a deeper relationship with me as we collectively enter into a deeper relationship with Christ.

(John Frey, business executive and youth ministry volunteer,
Disciples of Christ Church, Houston, Texas)

But who do you say that I am?

(Matthew 16.15)

When we help young people notice God, we're helping them attend to their experience of God. This is significant because the Bible is written by people who have encountered the Mystery of God. The authors of the New Testament sought to put into words the overwhelming experience of the Mystery of God that they had in Jesus Christ. This is the same pattern of spiritual growth we seek to facilitate among young people. We want young people to meet and experience the God that Jesus sought to reveal. We do this by creating settings and situations, time and space for young people to notice God's presence and love. The next step is to help them find words for their experience. An experience of God that isn't named or marked in some way is often lost or ignored. We need words or symbols for our experience of God in order to hold and savour the ways God is with us. In Christian formation we seek to help young people locate their experience of God within the language and experience of the Christian tradition, and then nurture their experience (their relationship with God) through practices of living that keep them available to God and others.

Possibly the most important skill in ministering with youth is knowing when to talk and when to listen. I've leaned heavily in this book on the importance of presence – being present not only to young people but to the God who moves within and amidst young people. I emphasize the importance of presence and listening because most teenagers experience adults as either absent or lecturing. Being a listening presence to youth and God are foundational skills in ministry – and often ignored in most youth curricula. However, I don't want to ignore the importance of speaking, of words. Adolescent spiritual formation means not only helping youth notice God, but helping them name this God as well. Good teaching is as important as good listening. It's just that good teaching, especially spiritual teaching, always begins with listening, with noticing, with waiting, with prayer and presence. It's out of our presence to young people and God that we're given words to speak and teach.

There are myriad books written on good teaching techniques, but here are some of the primary ways in which I seek to help young people find words for their experience of God:

1. Who do you say that I am?
It's interesting how many books and curriculum programmes try to explain Jesus to young people. Language is important. Theology is important. But these attempts to describe and define

Jesus are quite different from Jesus' own teaching style. Jesus is careful not to say too much about who he is. He uses strange terms like 'the Son of Man'. He speaks often of 'the Father', but says very little about his own identity; when he does speak of himself, he talks in parables and poetic language – bread, light, water and vines. 'Who do you say I am?' is the primary question he brings to Peter, and the question he seems to bring to all of us. 'Jesus is the question, not the answer', C. S. Lewis once wrote. Jesus relies on our experience, our encounters with him first, and then out of this he asks us, 'Who do you say that I am?'

When I work with young people, I try to be mindful of Jesus' teaching style. I try not to say too much. I try to create space, prayer exercises and service opportunities, and then ask them, 'Who do you say God is?' I try to help them lean into Jesus' life and then ask them to give me words for their experience. I hand out journals to write in. I sit them in circles and invite them to speak. I ask, 'Who is this God you experience?' or 'Who is this God you don't experience?' I question them, 'Who is Jesus?', 'How are you like Jesus?', 'How are you different from Jesus?' It's important for young people to speak the real words that express their under-standing and experience of God. This is true dialogue: to give space not only for youth to listen, but for youth to speak.

It was only my second Sunday as a volunteer when I asked the one question you don't ask in a junior high Sunday school room: 'If Jesus were here, do you think he would attend this church?' A hand shot up. It was Sam, the wary eighth-grade boy who rarely spoke. 'Of course not,' he barked, surprising everyone. 'Jesus would be bored here. He'd rather be out doing something. I never read in the Bible that he went to church. If he were here, he'd be helping people or checking out nature – that's what he did in the Bible. You'd never find Jesus sitting through all these long boring church services.'

The rest of the class sat silent in anticipation, basking in the awkward moment. I had the feeling I'd just crossed a line. The regular teacher gave me a sharp look that said, 'Thanks for undermining a year's worth of work!' Then she turned to Sam and said, 'You know, Sam, I think a lot of people in this church would be really hurt to hear you say that. Everyone works really hard. If they heard you say that Jesus wouldn't come here, I think they would feel devastated.'

Sam looked down, embarrassed, unsure of how to respond to this shaming. The other youth looked down as well. One mature, 13-year-old girl attempted to rescue us. 'I think Jesus would like to come to our church and listen to the sermons, since they're always about him.' Sam rolled his eyes, then slung his head down, avoiding eye contact with the leaders. In a soft, steady voice he offered, 'What kind of ego-maniac wants to come and hear people talk about how great he is? Is Jesus really that insecure?'

The leader went on the defensive. She spent the next 20 minutes explaining to Sam (and to herself?) the purpose of worship services, church institutions and life on planet Earth. Our ears full, we were all grateful when the worship service ended, freeing us from the classroom. I walked out with Sam. 'So be more specific,' I said, ignoring the past 20 minutes. 'If Jesus were in this town, where do you think he'd go?'

Sam picked up the conversation instantly: 'Wherever there is life. You know, wherever there's the opposite of boring.'

'What do you mean "the opposite of boring"?'

'You know . . . boring is like when you really don't need to be there; when it doesn't matter if you're there or not. Boring is the opposite of living. Jesus would be wherever people are really living, whether it's sad or happy – anything that's not, you know, like . . . flat.'

Curious, I stopped, turned to Sam and smiled. 'The way I see it,' he continued thoughtfully. 'Jesus was all about life. Doesn't he say somewhere that, "I am life . . ." or something?'

'So where do you find life?' I asked.

'That's easy – at the beach. If my mom wanted me to be close to God, she should take me out surfing each Sunday.' He paused and smiled. He liked this idea. 'You know you could make the whole thing a different kind of church. We could pray or something, read Scripture . . . you know, make it spiritual, and then we could go out and surf with Jesus. It could be like prayer. No talking or goofing around. Just riding the waves. Then everyone would come in and give thanks to God for the day.'

I stood there smiling at this image of surfing with Jesus. I looked at him taking in his excitement at this idea. 'That's a great image, Sam. I think you're right that Jesus wants to be where there's life. That's very cool.' He smiled at me, pleased with himself. 'Thank you for talking with me,' I said. He could tell I meant it. 'I'm going to think about that next time I feel really alive – I'm going to think about Jesus being with me.'

Three days after my encounter with Sam, I got an e-mail from his mother. 'For the first time in three years, Sam says he liked Sunday school. On the way home from church he told me he had a great conversation with you. He said he feels you're the only one who really understands him.' The truth was that I didn't really understand Sam. I was just beginning to know him. But I did listen to him. I kept from trying to sell him my own agenda. I allowed him to be himself. I delighted in his ideas and vision. I tried to just be present to him and give him a listening ear to explore his reflections on Jesus. I believe that Sam was really telling his mom that he enjoyed being heard. That he liked being able to express his ideas, and that in expression he discovered a new sense of himself and God.

Because of this interaction I began to engage Sam about the meaning of worship, about Jesus and his message of love. As I allowed Sam to express his ideas and experience of God, he was willing to listen to my thoughts, to Scripture, and to the tradition. We were in dialogue, searching side-by-side, wondering along with the first disciples, 'Who then is this, that even the wind and the sea obey him?' (Mark 4.41).

2. Let me tell you a story

Christians are people who tell stories. We tell stories of slavery and exodus, of faithfulness and pride, of sacrifice and betrayal. For Christians, the sacred stories found in the Bible are part of the great story of God, through Jesus, reconciling the world. But we do more than just tell these stories; we believe and live into these stories. We allow these stories to penetrate our understanding of life, to form and shape us, to guide and articulate our own experience. The stories of Scripture are windows into the nature of God and humanity and our relationship to one another. They are stories that help us repent, heal, learn, grow and stretch toward

God's love and wholeness. Christians believe Scripture locates us. It helps us to name our experience as well as to point us to deeper ways in which we can experience God's love and compassion for humanity.

Every time I lead a class or programme with young people, I try to tell a story from the Bible. I want the young people in my life to 'marinate' in the stories of Scripture, not only so they'll know that Jesus had 12 disciples and Moses was raised in Egypt – but so they can see how God is with us. I want them to hear the stories of the Bible until the Bible begins to read them – until they can interpret their situation through the images, situations and stories of the Bible.

For eight years I led week-long retreats entitled 'Sabbath' for youth ministers. Each retreat I would choose an account from Scripture in which someone encountered Jesus. This story would become the foundational passage for the week. Each day we would read a verse or two from the chosen passage during morning and evening prayer. We would lead prayer exercises on the story, and each morning one of the leaders would offer a simple meditation on the day's passage. By the end of the retreat, participants had heard the same story of an encounter with Jesus numerous times. They had prayed with it, studied it, worshipped with it and meditated on it.

I often noticed a change in people's experience of the story over the course of the week. For example, if we focused on the passage from Mark 1.40–45 in which Jesus heals a leper, I'd watch as people first encountered the story as a lesson: *Jesus is a healer. Those in need of healing should turn to Jesus.* As the week went on and they prayed with it over and over, it became more rich and textured. Suddenly people found themselves in the passage. They could feel themselves as the leper, bringing their sorrow and pain to Jesus. Or they found themselves as townspeople listening to the leper's story of healing, feeling jealous that they weren't the one touched by Jesus. Other times participants found themselves in the countryside with Jesus, avoiding the crowds or feeling compassion with Jesus as the leper pleaded for help. The way in which we continually sought to enter the story of Scripture helped people locate themselves in their lives with God and then pointed them toward new ways in which they could grow in relationship with Jesus.

We try to create the same atmosphere with young people. We don't just want them to read or hear the stories of Jesus, we want to allow them to enter into these stories. We give them invitations to find themselves in Scripture, to use the words and images of Scripture to deepen their experience of God. We ask them to tell us their feelings as the leper approaches Jesus. We invite them to place themselves imaginatively in the Scripture and tell us what they see. We ask them to tell us where they've seen or experienced the story in Scripture taking place today. All of these and other exercises help young people develop a vocabulary of faith – a way of navigating their lives with God, placing them in conversation with Christians who have travelled this journey for 2,000 years. As youth become familiar with the stories of faith, as they begin to see these stories illuminating their own life experiences, theological conversation comes naturally, grounded in what they've felt and known through the testimony of the biblical writers.

3. Testimony

Not only is it important for young people to hear the stories of Scripture, I also want to expose them to the stories of other Christians who follow Jesus. I remember leading a series of youth classes in which I'd invited different members of the congregation to meet with the young people and tell them about their own relationships with God throughout their lives. I brought in a retired sailor, a middle-aged real estate saleswoman, a young stockbroker, and a woman who ran a funeral home. All of them were asked to talk about their encounters with God and express why they called themselves followers of Jesus. The young people were riveted to hear stories of great doubt, debilitating tragedy, unanswered prayer and mystical experiences of Jesus' companionship. At the end of each testimony, I allowed kids to ask questions. It was easy to see that most of the youth's questions regarded their own struggles: 'Did you ever fall in love with someone who wasn't a Christian?', 'How could you keep following God after your mother died?', 'Did you ever do drugs when you were young?'

Young people not only want adults who will listen, but also

yearn to have adults who will engage them in truthful conversation. I find young people eager to hear the struggles and interior lives of adults. They want to hear the experiences of adult Christians who have struggled to make sense of tragedy, sin and temptation. They want to know how adults discern how to act in a secular world obsessed with sex, greed and violence. These testimonies and dialogues help give words and expression to the burgeoning struggles and experiences that exist in the lives of young people. They give them a perspective from which to make sense of their own yearnings and disappointments.

One time I helped organize a meeting where the young men in our youth group met with the adult men of the church, while the young women met with the adult women of our church. At each gathering the teenagers were invited to ask any question they wanted about what it was like to be an adult Christian. I facilitated the meeting between the young and older men. After a few minutes of awkwardness, one of the young men asked, 'How did you know what God wanted you to do with your life?' After some silence one man said he initially thought he'd be a grocer like his father, but then he decided to go to college. He studied engineering and became a civil engineer, but after a few years felt unsatisfied. So when a friend invited him to help start a software company, he quit his job. Similar stories of transition were told by other men, giving no clear picture as to how God had led each of them into his particular career.

A second young man then asked what they had learned about relating to women. There was an even longer pause. One man talked about feeling like he understood his wife when they first got married but then discovered he didn't know her at all; now, even in his fifties, he felt he was still learning how to relate to her. Others talked about divorce, about broken relationships, about how difficult it was to know how to relate to another person.

A third young man asked how they decided to commit to the Christian faith. Again we heard mixed stories of heartfelt commitments to Jesus followed by years of doubt and abandoning the faith. Some spoke of still feeling like they had one foot in the church and one foot out the door. As our time closed, I asked the young people to express what they had gathered from listening to the men. One boy looked thoughtful for a while and then said to the men, 'You guys don't have anything figured out, do you?' We all broke out in laughter. Then the same young man said, 'That's actually quite a relief. I feel so confused at times, and it seems so hard to know how God wants me to live. I've never told anyone that before. I always feel like I'm supposed to act confident – like I know what I'm doing and where I'm headed. It's such a relief to know I can be a Christian and not have everything figured out.' Hearing adults talk about the ambiguity and struggle of living the life of faith helped articulate the experience of many of the young people in that church and opened up further conversation between the generations in that community.

Creating settings where youth can hear the testimonies of other Christians, as well as express their own, helps them broaden and claim their experiences of God in new ways. Not only is it helpful for youth to hear the testimonies of other adult Christians, it's also extremely powerful for youth to hear the stories and testimonies of those Christians who we call saints. I often tell young people the story of St Francis and his struggle with his father. I tell them of St Antony and his sojourn in the desert after the death of his parents. I tell them about modern saints like Howard Thurman and his life of prayer and racial integration. All of this becomes both a comfort and an inspiration as their own experiences of faith are illumined and broadened through hearing the experiences of other lovers of God.

4. Beyond words

Of course, words aren't always needed to help youth name their experiences of God. Some of the most powerful expressions of faith in the Bible are actions or symbols with few words attached: the woman who bathes and anoints Jesus' feet; the haemorrhaging woman who touches Jesus' cloak; the poor widow who places two coins in the offering; the crowd waving palm branches as Jesus enters the holy city. These symbolic acts contain more than words can express and are, in many ways, more powerful than simple verbal expressions of faith. Just coming out of their childhood, language is not the first form of communication for many young people. It can be very helpful, from time to time, to invite youth to name their experiences of God in ways that don't rely on words.

In Chapter 11, I gave examples of prayer experiences that I've shared with youth that involve colours and creative media. These exercises can help young people explore as well as express their relationships with God in symbolic language. I've also found that the use of art media in prayer can help young people expand their understanding and relationship with God – especially for churched kids who can develop habits of expression and Christian understanding that insulate them from engaging God in new ways. I like to hang the artwork and prayer images created by youth in the places where I meet with young people. This not only honours their expression but begins to testify to the diverse relationships people have with God.

Inviting youth to find objects in nature to express their lives in God can also be revelatory. Once, after leading kids in a silent prayer exercise, I invited them to walk around the church grounds and find an object that best expressed their relationship with God. After 20 minutes or so, the youth returned. I encouraged people to share their objects with the group. One boy, who was quite shy and rarely spoke up, raised his hand and said, 'I found something that exactly expresses my relationship with God.' He then asked us all to gather around him. In his palm was a small purple flower bud. He held it out for all of us to see. He carefully closed his hand for a moment or two. When he uncurled his fingers, the flower, responding to the warmth of his hand, was opening. We all looked on in wonder as he smiled, pleased by this simple expression of his life in God.

For years my wife and I have designed interactive prayer spaces that allow young people and youth ministers to engage their relationship with God through a variety of symbols. We've designed prayer spaces according to particular lessons or conference themes that allow young people to pray in new ways. For example, one conference was focused on the different images of Jesus in the Gospel of John: light, bread, living water, the vine. We found a room that seemed quiet and comfortable. The room was low-lit with candles. In one corner we placed a planted vine with many branches. On a small placard we invited kids to pray about the parts of their lives where Jesus seemed absent – places where they wanted Jesus to 'abide' with them. Youth were then invited to take a ribbon and tie it on the vine branches as a symbol of their desire to stay close to Jesus.

Another corner was draped in thick black fabric. One red candle stood burning atop a small table surrounded by sand. 'I am the light of the world' was written at the base of the candle. Again, a small placard invited youth to come and pray about the dark places in their own lives and within the world. Youth were then encouraged to take a candle from the basket, light it, and place it in the sand next to the Christ candle. Another corner of the prayer room had a small pool of flowing water with lush plants growing at the water's edge. Pitchers of water were placed near the pool and people were invited to pray by the water's edge, reflecting on the ways in which God was seeking to pour living water into their lives and the life of the world. Seekers were then invited to pour a glass of cool water and drink it as a symbol of their desire to receive the life Jesus offers.

These kinds of creative, symbolic rituals and acts can help youth find new ways of uncovering and expressing their lives in God. Over time, rituals might emerge that become important to a particular group of kids. One church I worked with has a 'prayer net' – a large fishing net hung on one side of the youth room. At the end of each gathering, the youth share their prayer concerns with one another and pray. After each prayer concern is spoken, one of the youth ties a coloured ribbon on the net as a symbol of that prayer. When a prayer concern is too personal or painful for a youth to speak, the young person can simply pick up one of the ribbons and tie it to the net without saying a word. After a year the net was covered in ribbons – even though the group has no more than 18 kids. What does it mean for these kids to enter the youth room week after week and see this prayer net, slung heavy with prayers? What does it mean for young people to have the opportunity to express the prayers of their hearts without speaking a word? Maybe in this ritual they come closer to the Holy Spirit who prays within us, 'with sighs too deep for words'.

Faith takes time

Helping youth find their way into the Christian tradition takes time. All kids – and especially those with little church background – need lots of time and patience before Christian words and language give meaning to their unique experiences of life and the Mystery we call God. When you develop a relationship with a young person, it's important to understand that you are beginning a conversation that will last many years, even a lifetime. It may be that for the whole first year of your relationship with a young man, for example, all you'll talk about is basketball. Every time you try to change the subject, he tolerates it – but as soon as he gets the chance, he turns the subject back to basketball. Then the second year all you'll talk about is girls. Despite interesting Bible studies, spiritual exercises and inspiring worship services, you find that all he wants to discuss is the opposite sex. The third year you'll talk about his parents' divorce. Every conversation, no matter how informed and enlightened, will continually draw back to his relationship and troubles with his parents. The fourth year you'll find yourself discussing colleges and universities ad nauseam – entrance exams, grades and SAT scores. Then a year later, after he's left your ministry and gone off to college, you'll be standing in line at a fast-food restaurant and notice this same young man who used to be in your church. You sit down together and out of the blue he looks up at you and says, 'Do you ever wonder what life's about?'

For five years you've been talking about basketball, dating, divorce, parents and college. You've been waiting for five years to talk about the meaning of life. You've been waiting to talk about the Christian faith. Now, suddenly, because you were patient, because you were present, he's ready to talk to you about matters of the heart. Now he wants to listen to your understanding of life with God. Now he wants to find words that speak to his experience. He trusts you because he's known your patient companionship. After five years he trusts you enough to ask, 'What's all this Christianity stuff about anyway . . . and why do you go to this church?' And that's when it's time to talk. That's the time for words.

13

Nurturing

———➤•◄———

Before integrating contemplation, I did youth ministry very, very differently. We didn't eat dinner together. I planned the program to a T. I never ventured from the plan. I made it go, no matter who got anxious. (More often it was me.) Any distraction from the kids only made things worse as I ploughed through the programme. The youth ministry wasn't so open to intimacy, which comes from listening. I hardly noticed what was going on with the kids or advisors. I was often too busy with the agenda to even notice God's presence and rarely felt grateful in the ministry.

I'm slower now, and more intentional about what I do, although more often than not the intention is spontaneous. The intention is focused on one another and on God. I ask more questions – better questions – of God, of myself, of the kids. I go off on more tangents, which often lands us in a better place (paying better attention to that still small voice). I look for Belovedness. I might not be doing youth ministry any more, but I trust that God will work (in me, through me, and in spite of me, if necessary).

(Jen Butler, associate pastor,
Westminster Presbyterian Church, Eugene, Oregon)

Build your life as if it were a work of art.

(Abraham Heschel,
addressing the youth of North America, 1972)

Through prayer and presence we're better able to help kids notice and name their lives in God. Our next venture is to help each young person *nurture* this growing relationship of love.

It's naïve to believe our ministries can simply be times of sitting and listening to youth. Youth like to do stuff – and so do adults. The immediate question that most youth ministers, churches and parents face every week is, 'What are we going to do with the kids?' There are Sunday school classes, confirmation pro-grammes, youth group meetings and outings to plan. We can seek to be open and present to youth within these activities, but how do we create youth ministry programmes that aren't in direct contrast to the contemplative spirit we seek to foster? Once we begin to help kids notice and name their relationship with God, how do we create a ministry programme that nurtures and deepens this relationship of love?

Follow the thread

Up in the wine country north of San Francisco there lives an Orthodox priest who has spent the past 30 years of his life in prayer and solitude. A friend of mine spent a week with him in his hermitage. Except for morning and evening prayer, the two of them kept silence for seven days. At the end of the week, my friend, who is also Orthodox, went to the priest and asked him for a word – some offering of wisdom to help him on his journey of faith. The reclusive priest gave him three: 'Follow the thread.'

Many times I've wished God would wrap a rope around my waist and pull me where I need to go. Following Jesus is often murky, clouded with doubt and second-guessing. Ministry is no different. I often question whether the relationships, teaching and programmes I'm offering young people are responding to the needs of the youth and the movement of the Holy Spirit. I want clear signs and signals from God (as well as from the young people!) regarding how to act and lead, yet God continues to speak in a still, small voice. My experience is much closer to the guiding words of the praying priest – there seems to be a thin thread that runs through the noise and activity of my life and ministry. It's a thread I lose track of at times; a thread that requires me to slow down, look and feel in order not to lose it; a thread that, though thin and fragile, leads to life.

In ministry we seek to follow the thread. We seek to notice the ways in which God is moving within the ministry. We notice when kids are becoming responsive and alive. We notice where the need and hurt of young people are coming to the surface. We listen and talk and discern these experiences of God, and then we respond. Our programmes and activities always seek to grow out of the needs of youth and the movement of the Holy Spirit. This takes prayer, discernment, patience and creativity.

Sadly, most churches (and ministers) are so busy looking to imitate other, larger, 'successful' churches that they don't take the time to notice how God is uniquely present within their own congregations and young people. There is a lack of trust in their own gifts, prayer life and capacities to create a ministry with youth that would be effective.

To 'minister' comes from words meaning to 'attend' or 'serve'. The ministries we develop, the teachings we offer and the activities we do with youth always seek to come out of 'attending' to the needs of youth and the guidance of the Holy Spirit. This is what it means to 'follow the thread' in ministry. We notice the little places where life meets life – where God is breaking into the lives of our young people. We create programmes and curricula that follow the life that arises in the ministry.

Let me illustrate further. Below are three examples of ministries that nurture life in God because they respond to noticing the 'thread' of God's Spirit.

The Bread of Life

A friend of mine is married to a part-time pastor of a mid-sized church outside of Anchorage, Alaska. After much prodding by a committee of eager parents, she and her husband agreed to start a youth ministry at their church. They began with the traditional youth programmes – a teen Sunday school class and a mid-week youth group meeting. Parents, excited to have something for their teenagers, immediately sent their teens to each of these programmes. Unfortunately, the youth, many of whom had been dragged to Sunday morning worship throughout their childhood, had developed a resistance to anything church-related. During Sunday morning classes kids sat slouched and sleepy-eyed, their communication skills reduced to grunts and nods. At youth group meetings they disrupted any attempt to talk, study or practise anything connected to the Christian faith. Claiming it was 'too much like school', the youth informed the two youth leaders that they wanted youth group to be a social time to visit friends without 'all the boring stuff about God'.

Each week Winnie and her husband gathered people together to pray, listen, discern and respond to what they were noticing in the youth group. One week it became clear that they needed to interact with young people outside of the formal 'youth group' setting. Winnie began to seek kids out intentionally during potlucks and after worship when the youth hung out at the coffee table. One Sunday after worship she sat with two 13-year-old girls and began to talk about how they spent their Saturdays. Winnie mentioned that she liked to bake cookies. The two girls lit up, replying that they too loved to bake, but didn't get much time to do it. Winnie asked if the girls would bring their favourite recipes and ingredients to church the following Sunday, and after worship they would bake in the church kitchen. The girls were ecstatic.

The following week the two girls came to church carrying cooking supplies and baking ingredients, accompanied by a number of friends. After worship they all spent the whole afternoon creating different cookie concoctions and talked openly about their lives at school and at home. Winnie was so taken by the girls' openness and enthusiasm around baking that she asked if they would be willing to come to church early the following Sunday and bake bread for Communion. Again, the girls were excited by this idea – they'd never baked bread before – and agreed to come. The following Sunday the girls arrived just as the sun was coming up. They gathered in the church kitchen and began making the bread dough. They asked Winnie questions about Communion – where it began and why Christians practised it. They asked Winnie about her marriage to a minister and her relationship to the church. Winnie later told me this was one of the most significant discussions she'd had with young people at that church. They agreed to meet again to bake bread for the service.

Two years later Winnie continues to meet with a group of girls to bake bread for Communion. They often bake more than enough for the service and have begun taking the extra loaves to a local food shelter. When I called Winnie to ask her how it was going, she told me, 'The kids really see this as a service they offer the church and a way that they're living out their faith. On Sundays when I'm absent, they still show up and faithfully bake the bread. Last Sunday one of the church elders came into the kitchen and watched. He noticed that the kids were so absorbed in their baking that for several minutes no one spoke a word. They just quietly worked, kneading and shaping the bread. The morning bread-baking has become a significant part of their life with God.'

What's significant in this experience is that Winnie did not engage these kids in baking because of a book or programme. She wasn't trying to create a 'Baking Model of Ministry'. She simply began to pay attention to the young people, to listen to them, to notice where they came alive – and then followed that life. It turned out that in following that thread of life she discovered a way of ministering with these young girls that drew upon her own gifts and interests, a ministry 'programme' in which the youth felt free to explore their faith.

I was sick and you took care of me

Another friend of mine ministers with youth in an inner-city Episcopal church in Richmond, Virginia. The church holds an annual 'Community Action Fair', where various non-profit agencies that serve downtown Richmond set up booths at the church and share information about their programmes. Every year my friend Steve asks the youth to learn about the different organizations and then choose one to volunteer in for one day as part of their confirmation class. One year a representative of the children's ward of the Medical College of Virginia set up an information booth. A group of teens visited the booth and spoke with the volunteer from the Medical College. The children's ward was located just a block from the church, and the teens were surprised to learn that many of the children there were suffering from terminal illnesses.

The next week Steve gathered the youth and asked them to report which organization they had chosen to volunteer with. The young people who had met the representative from the Medical College of Virginia's children's ward spoke first. They told the rest of the group about the work of the children's ward, about the dying children and the college's need for volunteers to spend time caring for the children. These youth then proposed that the whole group serve at the ward, and that they not do it for a single day, but commit to doing it one Sunday a month for the next year.

For the next hour the youth and ministry team discussed the proposal. Finally, they agreed that they would volunteer together on a Sunday afternoon and see what it was like before making a year-long commitment. After the meeting the youth ministry leaders gathered for prayer and discernment. The leadership was feeling pessimistic about committing the youth group to spend one Sunday a month at the children's ward. Wouldn't this disrupt their teaching curriculum? Would parents be upset that their kids weren't in Sunday school? Would kids grow tired of volunteering? Volunteering at the hospital was a good deed, but was it really the mission of the youth ministry programme to be providing regular volunteers for the hospital?

For the next two weeks the youth ministry leadership sent out information about the volunteer day at the children's ward. When the day came to visit the ward, the youth programme had its highest turnout of the year. The teens arrived early to make cards and banners, plan games and collect storybooks. They walked to the ward en masse and, after a brief orientation with the hospital staff, spread out among the children's wing to sing songs, deliver cards, play games and befriend the sick children.

When it was time to leave, the youth gathered back at the church. They shared their experiences and then spent a long time praying about the children they had seen. After the youth left, the leadership met again. They prayed and listened and tried to discern how the Holy Spirit was seeking to guide the ministry. It was clear there was a deep, authentic sense of excitement from the kids about serving at the hospital. They reflected on Jesus' words, 'I was sick and you took care of me.' Then one parent serving on the ministry team remembered a classmate of the youth who had died of cancer when these young people were in grade school. She recalled the impact that the death of this young child had on the whole school. She shared that her own son still referred to it, even though many years had passed. 'I think these kids have a heart for dying children,' she reflected. 'I think these youth are called to serve these children, and we need to respond.'

The leadership decided to shift their curriculum (an expensive and popular one they had recently purchased). They would drop a lesson plan each month and replace it with a visit to the children's ward. They would help the youth design and plan a programme for the dying children. They would start a new teaching session on the Christian perspective on death and grief. They would contact the local hospice and train the youth in skills for being with dying children.

Three years later the Sunday morning youth programme at St Paul's Episcopal Church is still grounded in monthly visits to the nearby children's ward of the Medical College of Virginia. This ministry wasn't garnered from a book or programme. It came from a praying youth ministry community that was attentive to the youth and willing to respond to the nudging of the Holy Spirit. It was difficult, at first, to alter their plans and teaching design. But because the leadership was attentive, they knew that their real task was to follow Jesus' lead – and so they built a ministry around connecting the young people to the children in the hospital.

Bowling for Jesus

I spent three years working with a Lutheran church set back in the Cascade Mountains of Eastern Washington. It's a small but vibrant congregation with a commitment to social justice. In developing its youth ministry programme, the church had attracted a group of adults committed to contemplative prayer. They were interested in developing a contemplative approach to youth ministry, and attended various training events I co-led that presented many of the ideas and principles in this book. The church formed a small covenant community of adults who prayed together and followed the liturgy for discernment as they led the youth ministry. These adults had been deeply nurtured by contemplative prayer and wanted to share this way of prayer with the young people. They began to implement dramatic changes in the youth programme. They designed the youth room to be more of a prayer space with a small altar and candles. Teaching times became focused on exploring various traditional forms of contemplative prayer, games were replaced with long periods of silence and journalling. The adults were ecstatic at the new programme they had created and enjoyed the times of prayer and quiet with the youth. There was only one problem: the kids hated it.

Week after week as the youth leaders became more focused on teaching contemplative prayer, the youth became agitated and bored, and sometimes even fell asleep during long prayer periods. Some of the youth, frustrated with the silence, just stopped showing up to church. The adults, on the other hand, stayed committed to engaging kids in contemplative prayer. Many of them had undergone life-transforming experiences in prayer and deeply hoped the young people would have similar experiences. The tension came to a climax when the adults decided to make the annual summer mission trip a contemplative retreat in a New Mexico desert. The trip would be a Christian 'vision quest', much like Jesus' time in the wilderness before he began his public ministry. The kids would spend most of the week in solitude, silence and prayer.

The youth revolted; no one wanted to go on the trip. The leadership was surprised by the resistance and became confused as to how to respond. Should they insist they knew what was best for the teenagers and continue with the spiritual retreat? The following weeks were filled with uncertainty. The adult leadership continued to meet for contemplative prayer and discernment, they tried to deepen their attention to the youth, seeking to notice the moments when the youth were most alive. They talked, listened, prayed and sought to discern God's leading. As they shared they began to notice their own attachments and projections within the youth ministry. Painfully, they explored abandoning their plans for the contemplative retreat in New Mexico. This brought on a variety of responses. Some adults were grieved by the idea of giving up the retreat. As they deepened their reflection one woman bravely admitted that much of her energy around the retreat came out of her own desire to attend such an event. Painfully, she noticed that she wanted to lead a contemplative retreat in part because she wished that someone had taken her on a contemplative retreat when she was a teenager. Another woman realized she felt deeply called to a contemplative life, and the contemplative retreat was the primary reason she wanted to serve in the youth ministry – without it, she wasn't sure she was called to work with kids. Yet another volunteer talked about his impulse to finish what he'd started. He noticed how frustrated he felt to let go of an event he'd already spent many hours working on.

As the group continued to pray and take 'a long loving look at the real', they were forced to admit the retreat was more about them than the kids. When they told the youth the retreat was cancelled, the announcement was received with whoops and cheers. The adults noticed they soon felt relieved as well. But now they were faced with a programmatic hole. How would they organize the youth programme now that they had abandoned their contemplative curriculum? The volunteer leadership decided to let go of their previous agenda and simply look for signs of life and energy among the young people. To their dismay they recognized one primary place where the youth seemed to be most alive: at the bowling alley. Maybe it was from the weeks of silent prayer and study or because of the stress the youth felt at school and home – whatever the reason, each time they took the youth bowling, the kids seemed to light up. The adults noticed that the divisions between social groups quickly fell away as kids slapped each other high fives, cheered on team-mates, and sipped soda pop at the score table. Even the adults got into the act, laughing right along with the kids. At their next discernment meeting, everyone in the leadership group had to admit that the youth group seemed closer to living into the kingdom of God at the bowling alley than in a silent prayer exercise. They began to explore how they could make bowling a regular part of the group. The next week they told the youth they would go bowling once a month – with one twist. The group would have dinner together at the church beforehand and then walk to the alley together. The leaders felt dinner and the walk would provide greater opportunities for conversation and relationships with the youth.

At first the leadership felt guilty for offering a youth programme that felt like a night of 'fun and games'. But over time they discovered deeper issues that had previously gone unattended. There were new kids in the group who felt alienated; there were tensions between more privileged and less privileged kids. Through bowling and play the leadership began to realize that God had a deeper agenda – God wanted these kids to learn to become a community, to cross social and economic lines, to learn to pray and care for one another despite their differences.

Frank Rogers, Professor of Christian Education at Claremont School of Theology, served as one of the scholars involved in the Youth Ministry and Spirituality Project. After three years of observing the youth ministry in this congregation, he offered a summary of this Lutheran church's attempt to nurture faith in their young people:

> This church experimented with a contemplative approach to youth ministry. In doing so, they felt like total failures. The teens resisted the spiritual practices of prayer and retreat, and the adults, mired in frustration, scrapped the best contemplative curriculum they'd been able to find. But a contemplative approach to youth ministry does not entail teaching youth to become contemplatives. It entails a leadership committed to a contemplative process of its own that enables them to see ways of crafting programmatic action that authentically participates with God in nurturing life and faith in young people . . . Where other leaders, enamoured by their own creativity but blind to the cries of their youth, may have pushed their own agenda, these youth leaders let go of their own designs, listened deeply for the movements of God, and crafted actions that followed the pulse of their discernment. As such, they have much to teach us about the nature of authentic ministry.

Contemplative karaoke

It was just past 10 p.m. on the fifth night of a Youth Ministry and Spirituality Project retreat for youth and youth ministers on the campus of San Francisco Theological Seminary, and 17-year-old John Schwehn was going through a full-blown voice-change as he belted out the lyrics to the 1970s hit 'I Will Survive'. Ninety teenagers and adults sat whooping and clapping to the disco beat as John crowed to the karaoke machine and jigged something I'd call 'The Wounded-Chicken Two Step'. It was then, in the middle of this funky, ridiculous, joyful vamp, that I looked toward the back of the room and saw something familiar – something that caused me to cringe and look for cover. It was the face that appears regularly in my ministry with young people. This face can possess a variety of persons in vastly different settings, yet consistently evokes the same feelings of shame and punishment. It's the 'You're in *big* trouble' face – and it has followed me throughout my ministry.

On this particular night the face was found on two middle-aged seminary students who stood at the back of the room, their bodies rigidly defying the karaoke disco around them, as if to say, 'We will not boogie. We will not get down!' These two women met my eyes and gestured stiffly that I was to follow them outside. A few steps from the music they began to bear down, 'Do you know what time it is? Do you understand that some of us have classes in the morning? Don't you know that it's 8 minutes past the 10 p.m. sound ordinance?' They looked at me like I was a drug trafficker. I smiled sheepishly, apologized and promised to stop the karaoke. Satisfied but still disgruntled they asked me, 'So what are all these kids doing here on campus anyway?' I perked up, eager to change the tone of our conversation, and explained excitedly that this was a retreat for youth and youth leaders from across the country who were together exploring a 'contemplative approach' to youth ministry.

Their faces scrunched up like I'd poured spoiled cream in their coffee. 'Did you say "contemplative"?' one of them asked me incredulously.

'Yes,' I said, confused by her reaction.

'That,' she said, pointing to the room where two kids holding stuffed animals were now doing a night-club medley of *Veggie Tales* songs, 'is not contemplative!'

It's surprising to many, including the two seminary students on our campus, to find a ministry that claims to promote contemplative awareness leading a retreat that includes karaoke, body-surfing, ultimate Frisbee, and a game called 'Pony' in which kids and adults dance and sing, 'Here we go, gonna ride my pony, ridin' around on my big fat pony'. (The night after karaoke we were again busted by local residents and seminary students for playing Pony after 10 p.m.) What happened to silence? Where's the mystical prayer? What about journalling or solitude, Taizé music and *lectio divina?*

Western Christianity is a religion of dichotomies: you're either into spirituality or social justice, contemporary or traditional worship, educational or entertaining youth programmes, 'being' or 'doing'. Many in the Church, stuck in this either–or thinking, perceive that contemplative youth ministry is focused solely on prayer, silence and solitude. We associate contemplation with monk robes, candles and sitting Buddhas. Like the seminary students I encountered, it is difficult for us to imagine a 'spiritual' retreat (much less a 'contemplative' retreat) engaging kids in playful (and sometimes just plain goofy) activities.

The purpose of integrating contemplative presence in youth ministry is not to form kids into monks, nor is it to make us experts in contemplative prayer – it is to deepen our (youth and adults') awareness of God, others and self so that we might become fully alive. Jesus promises, 'I have come that you might have life', and our task as ministers is to give young people the space, relationships, experiences and knowledge needed to know how to hold that life.

Engaging kids solely in contemplative exercises is unnatural, because contemplative prayer does not lead to more contemplative prayer – it leads to authentic action. Activities within the youth ministry are no longer chosen frantically from resource books; instead the youth ministry becomes more responsive to the needs of the young people and the movement of the Holy Spirit. We begin to hold our programmes lightly, realizing they can be changed or discarded if they impede God's desire for love. We trust God more, knowing the Holy Spirit will be faithful within and maybe even despite our programmes. We give ourselves a break, and we have more compassion for lesson plans that fall flat and outings that don't live up to our hopes and expectations. Through greater prayer and presence, we notice the moments of connection between youth and God and try and build our programmes accordingly. Then, little by little, usually beneath our own awareness, the youth ministry begins to become alive with the Spirit of God. Increasingly there is real play filled with a sense of celebration and fun rather than competitiveness and hyperactive excitement. Discussions become engaging rather than alienating and prescriptive. Mission trips and social justice activities begin to spring from compassion instead of guilt. Even prayer experiences grow hospitable and ordinary, less pristine and 'otherworldly'. The ministry becomes something unique and natural to our community rather than a cookie-cutter, 'franchise' ministry imported from a mega-church.

As our relationships with youth become infused with prayer and relationship, as our ministries become more attentive to the movement of God, as we become more intentional about helping kids notice the way in which Jesus seeks to befriend them, our programmes and actions will become more natural and responsive to the real needs of kids – and more receptive to the deep desire of God that moves within us.

What *does* a contemplative approach to youth ministry look like? It looks like young people engaged in centring prayer as well as body surfing. It looks like youth doing *lectio divina* as well as critical study of the Bible. It looks like solitude as well as service projects, contemplative worship as well as disco karaoke. As Jesus points out again and again, it's not the method but the spirit – the love and awareness behind our activities – that makes them Christian.

14

Beyond fear

For me the key was learning to listen to God. Through the silence, spiritual direction, and a focus on contemplative listening to others, I began to listen in a totally different way. I began to listen for God in others, listen between the words, actions, and experiences with others to hear how God was present. I began to realize I must center myself in God so I can be present to God in all that I do. I began to understand that only when I was centered in him was I able to turn outward to others. In fact it was only as I centered myself in God that I began to reach out to others. This not only affected my work in youth ministry but probably had the greatest impact on how I related to my own family, my own teenagers at home.

(Bob Eiselt, accountant and volunteer youth leader, Bethlehem Lutheran Church, Bayport, Minnesota)

Adults have to show kids that they're loved by God. They can tell you as much as they want, but they have to show you in some way. They have to show you that no matter what you do, even if you drop lasagna on the couch, it'll be okay – like, 'We'll get over it. The couch was ugly in the first place. One more stain won't kill it. Life goes on.' This is so much easier than if they just keep telling you like, 'Hey, you're the beloved of God. Just believe it.' It's easier when they show it to you and you can do stupid stuff, and you can tell that they love you, no matter what.

(Amanda, age 15, Houston, Texas)

The first thing love does is melts . . .

(Thomas Aquinas)

I'm in a downtown church doing a youth ministry consultation. So far I've only met with the adult power brokers – session (the leadership board), elders, staff and parents. It's late on a Saturday afternoon, but I've asked the pastor if I could spend some time with the youth. Using a variety of tactics – pizza, threats and manipulation – the youth director is able to round up 30 kids. I tell kids the situation: 'I'm a youth ministry "expert" flown in from San Francisco. The parents and members of this church want to help you make this faith and this church your own. They don't know what to do. They want me to make recommendations. What do you want me to say to them?'

There is silence as the group measures my words against my appearance. There are some awkward glances at peers. Then a young girl, about 13, blurts out, 'Don't be afraid of us.' Other kids nod heads. 'Tell them to stop being afraid of us . . . We're their kids.'

As I spoke further with these kids, I began to get a greater sense of what they wanted to say to the adults. They were trying to say: 'Don't hold us at arm's length. Don't keep us distant. Don't pawn us off to a programme, curriculum, or outside expert. After all, we're your children. We eat with you at your table. We listen in on your conversations. We sleep in the rooms next to yours. We're not an outside group. We come from your bodies. We're as close as the deepest hope within you – as close as your very hearts. Don't be afraid of us. Yes, we get frustrated when we don't understand your words or actions, and when you don't understand ours. Yes, we have energy and like to move, talk, and play. Yes, we are irritating and contrary at times – but we're trying to find our way in the world. We're trying to test reality, find its limits – see what ground is sandy and what ground is solid enough to stand on. We're really no different than you. Don't be afraid of us. We don't know who we are. But meanwhile we need someone to accept and accompany us. We need love and companionship, because although our bodies are different, at the level of the heart we're really a lot like you.'

Don't be afraid of us. What does it mean? It means staying close to our young people. It means being vulnerable and open to young people. It means staying close to our own hearts, the temples where God's Spirit dwells. It means ending our search for an outside fix, a mediator between youth and us. It means churches facing their children on their own, with nothing but their own desire for relationship and their own testimony and practice of life. It means that the solution to the 'youth ministry question' can only be found with and among young people. It means trusting that the Mystery of God that works within each of us will birth new openings to life and relationship.

*   *   *

Four years ago the leaders of First United Methodist Church in Valparaiso, Indiana were faced with a crisis involving skateboarders. It seemed the sidewalks, paved parking lot and cement steps of the church had become a popular gathering place for local teen skaters. Every day kids in baggy clothes and tilted baseball caps pushed their wheels across the church property, leaped and flipped their boards across the church sidewalks, and then spent the late afternoon grinding their 'trucks' (the metal axle joints underneath their boards) against the cement steps. Soon the cement began to crumble and break. Upset by the damage to church property, the church leadership decided to replace the steps, install protective devices into the cement to prevent skating, and post signs outlawing loitering and skateboarding.

The youth director and the covenant community of adults who served the youth ministry went to the church leadership and asked them to reconsider their decision. For three years the group had met each week to pray and seek guidance on serving kids in the community. They asked if the leadership might see the presence of youth as a blessing and, instead of asking them to leave, find ways to develop and deepen relationships with them. After weeks of prayer and discernment, the church leadership decided to reverse its decision. It left the crumbling and scuffed cement steps and removed the signs outlawing skateboarders and loitering. The pastor told me, 'We decided to let the church have the ugliest front steps in town.'

The next day leaders of the church met with the teen skaters and informed the youth of the church's decision. They told the skateboarders they were welcome to skate on the church property and let them know they were welcome to use the other church facilities as well. They gave the kids a tour of the church building and showed them where the bathrooms and kitchen were located. They took the youth into the church office and introduced them to the staff.

If you want to know what it means to share the presence of Jesus with young people, if you want to know more than I can tell you in this book, then drive an hour east of Chicago to Valparaiso, Indiana. Go spend an afternoon sitting on the kerb across the street from the Methodist church. Then watch as kids come skating up to the steps, leaping and twirling, crashing their boards against the concrete in acrobatic feats of life and energy. Sit and watch as the church secretaries, the book-keeper, the maintenance and pastoral staff walk up the crumbling steps. Watch as they stop to say hello. Watch as they converse with the scruffy street skaters. Notice as they take time from their work to applaud as a boy shows off an especially difficult spin on his board. Sit and don't say a word. Just watch and listen to the whirr of the wheels on the pavement. Watch the young people running in and out of the church to get water and use the bathroom and then see. See if you don't find those crumbling steps beautiful.

Notes

1 Almost any study in the past 20 years on adolescent health and religiosity makes this claim. See Chap Clark, *Hurt* (Baker Academic, 2004), or the recent work of the National Study of Youth and Religion, particularly Christian Smith with Melinda Lundquist Denton, *Soul Searching: The Religious and Spiritual Lives of American Teenagers* (Oxford University Press, 2005).

2 This summary was in the 2004 spring newsletter of the Search Institute. For more information from the Search Institute, see www.search-institute.org

3 *Soul Searching: The Religious and Spiritual Lives of American Teenagers*, p. 182.

4 Gustav Reininger (ed.), *Centering Prayer in Daily Life and Ministry* (Continuum, 1998), p. 130.

5 The term 'resting in God' comes from sixth-century mystical theologian, Gregory the Great.

6 Forms of centring or silent prayer can be found in the writings of the early Desert Fathers and Mothers, Julian of Norwich, John of the Cross and other mystical theologians, and are most clearly articulated in the anonymously written fourteenth-century devotional, *The Cloud of Unknowing*. One of the 'founders' of centring prayer, M. Basil Pennington, sees centring prayer as a direct outgrowth of *lectio divina* in *Centering Prayer: Renewing an Ancient Christian Prayer Form* (Doubleday, 1980). For more on the history and tradition of centring prayer, see 'The Christian Contemplative Tradition and Centering Prayer', in Gustav Reininger (ed.), *Centering Prayer In Daily Life and Ministry*.

7 These guidelines are modified from Thomas Keating's description of the Method of Centring Prayer found in many of his writings, including *Open Mind, Open Heart* (Element, 1986) and *Centering Prayer in Daily Life and Ministry*.

8 From 'The Nature of Our Humanity' lecture given to the Houston Medical Group, Houston, Texas, April 1999.

9 Richard Rohr, *Everything Belongs: The Gift of Contemplative Prayer* (Crossroad, 1999), p. 33.

10 Excerpt from 'The Ministry of Listening' in John Dobbenstein (trans.), *Life Together* (Harper & Row, 1954), pp. 97–99.

11   In the Orthodox tradition icons are sacred paintings that serve as 'windows' through which we see and experience God. Sometimes our memories or experiences can serve the same function.

12   Parker Palmer, *The Active Life* (Harper San Francisco, 1991).

13   Jean Vanier, founder of L'Arche, a faith-based international network of more than 100 communities in 30 countries for people with disabilities. *Becoming Human* (Paulist Press, 1999), p. 22.

14   *The Spiritual Exercises* was written for retreat leaders and spiritual directors who had experienced the 30-day retreat. It is not recommended reading without first experiencing the exercises with a knowledgeable retreat leader.

15   Dennis Linn, Sheila Fabricant Linn and Matthew Linn, *Sleeping with Bread* (Paulist Press, 1995). These two questions come from the Linns' simple description of the awareness examen and its application to daily life. The Linns offer other questions such as, 'When today did you receive and give the most love?'

16   Luke 17.21.

17   *Soul Searching: The Religious and Spiritual Lives of American Teenagers*, p. 185.

18   This statement comes from Dr Andy Dreitcer, in a presentation on discernment, February 1998. Andy served as the co-founder and co-director of the Youth Ministry and Spirituality Project from 1997 to 2000.

19   I borrow this phrase from Parker Palmer in *A Hidden Wholeness: The Journey Toward an Undivided Life* (Jossey-Bass, 2004). Palmer defines a 'circle of trust' as a group whose intent is to make it safe for the soul to show up and offer us guidance.

20   Two helpful resources in regard to communal discernment in ministry are Suzanne G. Farnham, Joseph P. Gill, R. Taylor McLean and Susan M. Ward, *Listening Hearts: Discerning Call in Community* (Harrisburg, PA: Morehouse Publishing, 1991); and Suzanne G. Farnham, Stephanie A. Hull and R. Taylor McLean, *Grounded in God: Discernment for Group Deliberations* (Morehouse Publishing, 1996). Both books have excellent guidelines for ministry groups.

21   Alan Jones, *Exploring Spiritual Direction: An Essay on Christian Friendship* (Seabury Press, 1982), p. 8.

22   Works on prayer such as Daniel Wolpert's *Creating a Life with God* (Upper Room, 2003), Tilden Edwards' *Living in the Presence* (Harper San Francisco, 1987) and (written specifically for youth ministers) Tony Jones' *Soul Shaper* (Youth Specialities, 2003) all contain exercises and prayers that can be helpful in awakening young people to the love of God.

23   See *Sleeping with Bread*.

24   March 1990, in a series of talks and discussions in Germany, some of which are recorded in *Simplicity: The Art of Living* (Crossroad, 1991).

Appendix 1

The two charts in Appendix 1 are visual descriptions of contemplative youth ministry that were developed within the Youth Ministry and Spirituality Project.

Three Approaches to Youth Ministry is a simple comparison of the roles, theology and objectives of contemplative youth ministry when compared to the 'consumer' and 'content' approaches to youth work. The 'consumer' approach refers to those models of ministry that focus on entertaining youth, thereby reflecting the values and mores of the market culture. The 'content' approach describes an educational model solely directed to the transfer of religious information. All of these descriptions are quite general; any youth ministry programme will be a complex mixture of all of these approaches (and others). Yet the comparison helps to expose the intention of a contemplative approach to youth ministry in contrast to other forms of ministry.

The Contemplative Ministry Cycle charts the movements and tensions I have observed within a variety of congregations as they have engaged in contemplative youth ministry. Again, this cycle is a general description of the experience of contemplative youth ministry within a congregation. In real life it appears much more complex and messy. And yet, over time these movements and tensions do become more and more clear within youth ministries that seek to integrate contemplative prayer and communal discernment.

Three approaches to youth ministry

	Consumer	*Content*	*Contemplation*
Rooted in	Anxiety/fear.	Complacency.	Love.
Theology	Faith is good fun.	Faith is conformity. Dogmatic literacy.	Faith is an ongoing relationship.
Minister	Programme. Director/professional. Christian.	Instructor/person with answers.	Spiritual director (points to the presence of God). Theologically and biblically informed disciple.
Volunteers	Chaperones.	Classroom aides.	Seekers, mentors, elders.
Teaching	Civic values.	Religious information/ indoctrination.	Way of Jesus/ Christian living.
Practices	Passivity, entertainment, consumerism.	Conformity, memorization, regurgitation.	Action rooted in prayer and theological reflection.
People	Religious consumers.	Potential institutional members.	Spiritual seekers, developing a way of life.
Constituency	Board members/ status quo.	Religious institutions.	Body of Christ/ the living God.

The contemplative ministry cycle

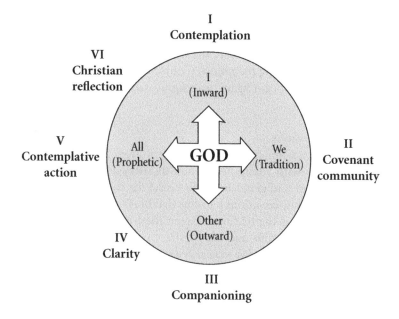

I **Contemplation.** Sabbath and prayer help us pay attention to the presence of God in our life and the life of the ministry.

II **Covenant community.** We join with others to tend the Spirit, deepen our discernment of God's call and share the burdens of ministry.

III **Companioning.** We move out of prayer and community to accompany young people. Young people draw us out of prayer into service and care.

IV **Clarity.** As we pray and relate to young people, we begin to gain clarity as to how the Holy Spirit is calling us to act. This is the moment for discerning how (what programmes, relationships, activities?) we are called to minister with youth.

V **Contemplative action.** Grounded in God and community we now begin to take action either on behalf of youth or with youth in service to a hurting world. Our programmes and ministries are developed at this stage.

VI **Christian reflection.** We reflect on our actions in light of Scripture and our Christian tradition. We name how the Spirit is moving or blocked through our programmes and actions.

I **Contemplation.** We start the cycle again. Returning to the Source – offering the ministry, ourselves, and our actions up to God. We begin again, waiting on God for guidance and renewal.

The inner tensions

As we live into this ministry cycle, our prayer, community life, relationships with young people and ministry activities deepen, growing closer and closer to God's vision for the ministry. Over time, we may notice various tensions that break us open, bringing new life. There is the tension between the I and the Thou – my individual prayer life and my desire to move out of myself towards young people. We may also notice that as we increase our interactions with young people, we are in greater need of silence and prayer.

There is the tension between the ministry team, the covenant community that tends the tradition of the congregation, and the prophetic actions that arise in relation to young people. Ministries with youth will inevitably challenge the traditions and practices of the sponsoring congregation.

These are the tensions that make up the Christian life – between silence and service, the worshipping community and the suffering world. As we live these tensions our own agendas are broken down. We become more aware and available to God's vision within our ministry as well as our individual and collective lives.

Appendix 2

Below is a simple description of the movements of the liturgy for discernment. It is helpful when teaching the liturgy to volunteers.

Liturgy for discernment

Ritual
Silence, a song, lighting of a candle . . . some ritual that helps us recognize the presence of God.

Relating
Checking in. Attending to one another. 'How are you?'

Receiving
Attending to God through prayer, either *lectio divina* or the awareness examen.

Ruminating
Each person shares what they noticed during the prayer.

Reflecting
Touching into our call/mission. The group answers the following question: 'Given what we've heard and shared, what is God's call to us?'

Responding
Out of listening, we do our work. We look at our business items.

Returning
Closing prayer. Offering ourselves/efforts to God.

Appendix 3

---•◦•---

Youth ministry volunteers' retreat

The following retreat outline was developed within the Youth Ministry and Spirituality Project. It is designed as a one-day gathering for youth ministry volunteers as they prepare to begin a year of ministry with youth.

Purpose

This one-day retreat has the following objectives:

1 To begin building relationships among the ministry team.
2 To help individuals identify and deepen their call to this ministry.
3 To begin to discover the collective identity and the unique vision that God is calling the group to undertake.
4 To help volunteers understand their roles and the way in which they will function as a group.
5 To begin to do some basic planning/organizing for the year.

Setting

Choose a setting that will have limited distractions. Sometimes going to a retreat centre or even spending a day at a different church allows a new openness and awareness among the group. Try not to hold this retreat at your church – it may be too distracting for staff and other members, and too tempting to make phone calls or fiddle with other tasks and projects during break times.

Supplies
Bible.
Copy of 'Liturgy for Discernment' (Appendix 2) for each person.
Pens and paper for each person.
Crayons and drawing and/or construction paper.
Clay (optional).
Flipchart or whiteboard with pens.
Candle.
Matches.
Tape recorder or CD player with contemplative/spiritual/reflective music.
Snacks/drinks.
Lunch (or plan for lunch out).

Schedule
8 a.m.   Retreat facilitator should arrive and set up room.

9 a.m.   Volunteers should arrive.

9–9.20 a.m.   Snacks, coffee, informal conversation.

9.20 a.m.   *Begin retreat.* Opening prayer or ritual to begin time together.

9.25 a.m.   Facilitator should go over schedule and briefly outline the purpose of the retreat (see above).

9.35 a.m.   *Ritual. Relating.* Check-in. Time for people to answer, 'How are you today?' (This may take time if you have a large group . . . or you may want to break into smaller groups.)

9.50 a.m.   *Lectio divina (receiving).* After everyone has shared, invite the group to a time of prayer. (You should already have a passage chosen for this exercise. Some good passages that focus on call and ministry include Jeremiah 1.4–8; Isaiah 43.1–7; Mark 10.13–16; Mark 4.1–9; Luke 4.16–21.) Explain how you are going to lead this prayer. For example you might say:

In a moment I'll invite us to spend some time in God's presence. We'll have a couple of minutes of silence, then I'll read the Scripture passage three times. As I'm reading, listen for a word or phrase that seems to stand out, that seems addressed to you, like it's in bold. If a word comes to you, ignore the rest of the reading and just begin to meditate on that word, repeating it over and over within yourself. See what images and insights come to you. After reflecting on the word, you may find yourself drawn to simply rest in the silence . . . enjoying God's presence, grateful for this time of prayer.

We'll have about five minutes of silence after the second reading. [For people who have never experienced contemplative prayer, five minutes can be plenty of time. Add more time, however, if you sense the need for a longer period of quiet.] *After five minutes I'll invite us to draw our attention back to the group and then I'll ask each of us to share what, if anything, has come to us during the prayer. Any questions? . . . Then let us pray.*

Lead the prayer, allowing for five minutes of silence. At the end of the five minutes invite people to offer thanks to God and then draw their attention back to the group.

10.05 a.m.   *Ruminating.* Invite people to share the word that came to them and any insights or noticings that came out of the prayer. Remind them to speak as simply and succinctly as possible if the group is large.

10.20 a.m.   *Reflecting.* Call. Ask the group, 'Given everything we've heard and shared what is our call (God's invitation to us) this morning? What is God saying to us this morning as a group?' The purpose of this question is for the group to begin to notice common images and insights from the sharing and begin to notice common ways that the group is being called to serve/live. Also be prepared that there may not be any connections.

10.30 a.m.   *Break.*

10.45 a.m.   *Prayer exercise.* Invite the individuals in your group to engage in a prayer exercise with colours. Explain that this is not an art exercise but a time of prayer without words. You might say the following:

The purpose of the prayer is to listen for the ways in which God is seeking to relate to you at this time in your life. We are listening for how God is calling each of us to live so that we might be clearer as to how this ministry is part of God's overall call in our lives. We'll do this through creating images of our individual lives. In a minute I'll invite you to a time of silent prayer. In this silence I want you to take a piece of paper and some colours, and then find a place by yourself somewhere in the room (or facility). Ask God to give you an image of your life at this time. It may contain images of different aspects of your life right now . . . it may be more impressionistic . . . just colours and designs. Don't try and force anything; just let the images or colours come as you pray. [You may want to use this time to explain your own understanding of call. Refer to some of the readings, notes from the inservice, or explain your own understanding or experience of call in order to give the group some ideas on what to pay attention to.]

11.15 a.m.   Have the group gather and share the images and reflections from the prayer. Ask them:

1 What do you notice about your relationship to God in this picture?
2 What seems to be God's invitation or call as you look at this image of your life?
3 How is this ministry part of your life as you look at this image?

11.45 a.m.   At the end of the sharing ask, 'Are there any common themes in our sharing?' Spend some time discussing this question.

12.30 p.m.   *Lunch.*

1.45 p.m.   *Covenant.* Create a covenant of how you hope to work together. Present some of the commitments in the original calling (hours per week, meeting times, etc.). Explain the roles of volunteers and the purpose of the ministry team. Create a 'working covenant', a document that can be revised as the group engages in the ministry.

3 p.m.   *Break.*

3.15 p.m.   *Liturgy for discernment.* Hand out copies of 'Liturgy for discernment' and go over the steps of the meeting. You might reflect on how many of these steps have been experienced and incorporated into the retreat this day.

4 p.m. *Business.* Go over any agenda items . . . whatever tasks the group has for the ministry.

5 p.m. *Awareness examen.* End with an awareness examen over the day. For what moment do people feel most grateful?

5.30 p.m. *Returning.* Closing prayer.

6 p.m. *Dinner together.* It might be nice to have dinner, inviting the families of the ministry team in order to see the larger context in which this ministry operates.

Appendix 4

———➤•◄———

Guidelines for leading a prayer exercise with youth

The following comments and instructions evolved within the Youth Ministry and Spirituality Project as an aid when leading contemplative prayer with young people. Youth leaders within the project found these guidelines to be a helpful reminder as they designed prayer experiences.

Hospitality

Before you begin, dedicate your efforts to God and trust that God will work through the exercise. Remind yourself that the prayer is not about you, it's about God.

Have a set order and time for the exercise. Have all materials ready and available. Think through how the exercise will take place. Create a welcoming space for the prayer to take place. Pay attention to the senses . . . is there beauty? Does the space help draw attention to God's presence?

Invitation

Describe the whole exercise to young people in simple terms. Make sure everyone understands how the exercise will proceed. Try and have an 'experimental' tone during the invitation to prayer. Say something to the effect of, 'We're going to try an experiment in prayer. It may or may not be the way in which you pray, you might feel a little strange or uncomfortable with the silence, but I want to ask that you give it a try and see what happens. God can surprise us sometimes and show up in ways that we don't normally expect.'

Sometimes it's helpful to talk about the different ways we're in relationship with other people: we talk, we listen, we do things together, and sometimes we're just together, without words – try and help youth see that the prayer is similar to listening or just being with a friend without words.

Be sure to acknowledge difficulties. Acknowledge what may not 'work'. Make sure kids understand that there is no 'right' way to experience the exercise. I often say something like, 'Sometimes when we pray it's difficult to focus – our minds are moving too fast, we're tired, or maybe this just isn't the best way for us to pray. That's OK. Don't get stressed if you're having a hard time with this exercise. Just simply say within yourself, "God, I want to be with you right now", and let everything else fall away.'

Allow the group to get physically comfortable before you start.

Prayer
Lead the group in a centring exercise as you begin the prayer. Darken the room and light a candle to help them focus their attention. Have them pay attention to their breathing, relax their body and turn their attention toward God. You may prefer to have the group sing a simple chorus to help ready their hearts for prayer.

Invite the youth to dedicate the time to God. Remind them that it is their desire to be with God that is most important in prayer. Then simply allow the group to spend some time in prayer. Make sure you pray along with the young people. Trust that God is at work – try and ease up on monitoring the kids. If there are kids who become disruptive, speak the truth in love – call them back to prayer using an economy of words. In silence we often worry that nothing is 'happening'. Remember that silence is God's first language – try to let go of worrying about whether the exercise is 'working'.

At the end of the prayer time, gently invite youth to offer thanks to God for whatever occurred during prayer. Have an appropriate closing for the prayer (maybe the Lord's prayer or a simple song) and transition back to the group.

Testimony

Sometimes at the close of the prayer it might be appropriate to invite the youth to express their prayer experience through some physical expression or ritual: lighting a candle, placing a rock before a cross, etc. At other times it might be important to have kids spend time journalling their experience. Even after journalling it's helpful to invite youth to speak their experience within the larger group. It's good for kids to hear the variety of experiences within prayer. This also gives the leaders a chance to answer questions and respond to theological or spiritual issues that arise.

If you give kids a chance to talk about their experience, make sure you respond with open-hearted, non-judgemental remarks – remember that you don't know what God is doing within these young people, so be open. If you're concerned about a young person's prayer experience, follow up with him or her privately. Let kids know that this exercise may not work for everyone – it's just an exercise, it's not God. Allow people to talk about 'flat' experiences as well: 'I fell asleep', 'I couldn't focus', 'I had no sense that God was present in this prayer'. Such experiences are common for both youth and adults.

Let kids know that their prayer experience, whether enlightening or flat, is part of trying to be in relationship with God and is common among Christians throughout history. Remind them again that their desire to be with God is what's most important and pleasing to God.

References

Bonhoeffer, Dietrich, *Life Together* (Harper & Row, 1954).

Edwards, Tilden, *Living in the Presence* (Harper San Francisco, 1987).

Farnham, Suzanne G., Stephanie A. Hull and R. Taylor McLean, *Grounded in God: Discernment for Group Deliberations* (Morehouse, 1996).

Farnham, Suzanne G., Joseph P. Gill, R. Taylor McLean and Susan M. Ward, *Listening Hearts: Discerning Call in Community* (Morehouse, 1991).

Jones, Alan, *Exploring Spiritual Direction: An Essay on Christian Friendship,* (Seabury, 1982).

Jones, Tony, *Soul Shaper* (Youth Specialities, 2003).

Keating, Thomas, *Open Mind, Open Heart* (Element, 1986).

Kelly, Thomas R., *A Testament of Devotion* (Harper San Francisco, 1996).

Lawrence, Brother, *The Practice of the Presence of God* (Spire, 1958).

Linn, Dennis, Sheila Fabricant Linn and Matthew Linn, *Sleeping with Bread: Holding What Gives You Life* (Paulist Press, 1995).

May, Gerald, *The Awakened Heart* (Harper Collins, 1991).

Merton, Thomas, *Thoughts in Solitude* (Rosetta, 2005).

Nouwen, Henri, *The Inner Voice of Love* (Image, 1998).

Palmer, Parker, *The Active Life* (Harper San Francisco, 1991).

Palmer, Parker, *A Hidden Wholeness: The Journey Toward an Undivided Life* (Jossey-Bass, 2004).

Palmer, Parker, *Let Your Life Speak* (Jossey-Bass, 2000)

Pennington, M. Basil, *Centering Prayer: Renewing an Ancient Christian Prayer Form* (Doubleday, 1980).

Reininger, Gustav (ed.), *Centering Prayer in Daily Life and Ministry* (Continuum, 1998).

Rohr, Richard, *Everything Belongs: The Gift of Contemplative Prayer* (Crossroad, 1999).

Rohr, Richard, *Simplicity: The Art of Living* (Crossroads, 1991).

Smith, Christian with Denton, Melinda Lundquist, *Soul Searching: The Religious and Spiritual Lives of American Teenagers* (Oxford University Press, 2005).

Vanier, Jean, *Becoming Human* (Paulist Press, 1999).

Wolpert, Daniel, *Creating a Life with God* (Upper Room, 2003).

Printed and bound by CPI Group (UK) Ltd, Croydon, CR0 4YY

25/03/2025

14647344-0002